Reshaping Rural Ministry

Reshaping Rural Ministry

A Theological and Practical Handbook

Edited by
James Bell,
Jill Hopkinson and
Trevor Willmott

CANTERBURY
PRESS
Norwich

First published in 2009 by the Canterbury Press Norwich
Editorial office
13–17 Long Lane,
London, EC1A 9PN, UK

Canterbury Press is an imprint of Hymns Ancient and Modern Ltd
(a registered charity)
St Mary's Works, St Mary's Plain,
Norwich, NR3 3BH, UK

www.scm-canterburypress.co.uk

British Library Cataloguing in Publication data

A catalogue record for this book is available
from the British Library

978 1 85311 953 8

Typeset by Regent Typesetting, London
Printed in the UK by CPI William Clowes Beccles NR34 7TL

Contents

Preface

Every aspect of the church's ministry arises from the *missio Dei*, the mission of God for his world. The changes and challenges confronting the rural church have stimulated a renewed reflection on what mission and evangelism mean in these contexts. The characteristic themes of presence, service and proclamation lead to an appreciation of distinctive approaches to mission which are both implicit and explicit within the rural context.

The countryside is not the rural idyll many may imagine, but a place where global challenges of food production, increasing energy costs and climate change are most keenly felt. Sustaining rural communities raises major issues: affordable housing, transport, jobs, economic vitality and the provision of services. Alongside these key concerns, the care of the environment continues to be a major item on the political agenda.

The rural church, with its abiding presence through countless generations in almost every rural community, is an essential part of the fabric of social and communal life. This is symbolized by the church building that is so much part of the story of each place and the offering of worship connected with the cyclical nature of life. When other public services have been withdrawn, the rural church steadfastly remains as a sign of integrity, value and hope. Pastorally and prophetically, the rural church community engages with the issues facing rural neighbourhoods and the individuals affected by them.

Given this demanding context, rural ministry is at the cutting edge of ministry, reshaped and reinvigorated for a changing world. Older models of ministry have proved unsustainable, not least through the grouping together of increasing numbers of parishes. This has necessitated the reappraisal of the role of the ordained and the reaffirmation of the calling of the whole people of God. Ecumenical partnerships are a further expression of the pioneering development of collaborative working. In circumstances where the parish church is the only church in a place, rural churches offer welcome and hospitality by being open to all people and by affirming diverse traditions. Relatively small congregations present the opportunity for celebration, community, intimacy and a depth of shared spirituality. Much can be learnt by the wider church from rural churches' creativity in responding to challenging circumstances as well as in their thirst for community, the opportunities for partnership and the potential of spiritual development.

I am grateful to the Rural Bishops' Panel of the House of Bishops for sponsoring this much needed and stimulating exploration of rural mission and ministry.

I warmly commend this book to all those engaged in rural ministry, to the wider church, and especially those who are exploring a vocation to ministry in rural areas.

Dr John Sentamu
Archbishop of York
2009

The contributors

James Bell is Bishop of Knaresborough in the Diocese of Ripon and Leeds, where major responsibilities include evangelism, church growth and rural affairs. Previously Director of Mission in the same diocese, he has served in chaplaincy, parochial and training contexts. He was born and bred in the Eden Valley in Cumbria and has a significant farming family background.

Joanna Cox is National Adviser in Lay Discipleship and Shared Ministry for the Church of England. In the past she has taught in schools in inner-city London and in rural Africa. Other jobs have included helping to prepare adults for inter-cultural mission and for local ministry in both rural and urban areas. These experiences have helped her recognize the significance of the local context, and that the church must avoid approaches that assume that one size fits all.

Jill Hopkinson is National Rural Officer for the Church of England, based at the Arthur Rank Centre in Warwickshire, the churches' rural resources centre. She originally trained in ecological and agricultural sciences and now advises on, and provides training for, rural churches and communities. She has written and edited a number of publications for rural churches, including *Country Way* magazine.

Jeremy Martineau has been an Anglican priest for over 40 years and was awarded the OBE for services to rural communities. He was chairman of ACRE and the first National Rural

Officer for the Church of England until 2003. He is Director of Studies for the Centre for Studies in Rural Ministry, a partnership between the Arthur Rank Centre and St Deiniols' library. He has written and edited several books on the work of the church in rural areas.

Leslie Morley has been the Rural Officer for the Diocese of Ripon and Leeds since 1999. He is a volunteer with Farm Crisis Network, an Agricultural Chaplain and Honorary Chaplain to the Yorkshire Agricultural Society. He has been involved in bringing together public and voluntary sector organizations concerned with issues of rural stress. He is also one-half of the 'Cooking Canons' duo, '*Cooking in Heaven's Kitchen*', which raises awareness of local food and farming, and promotes the work of the Royal Agricultural Benevolent Institution.

Amiel Osmaston has had lifelong family involvement in forestry, farming and rural life. She has spent nine years in full-time parish ministry, and then trained clergy at Ridley Hall, Cambridge. As diocesan Ministry Development Officer, first in Cheshire and now in Cumbria, she is responsible for growing laity and clergy in ministry and enabling collaborative leadership.

Martyn Percy is Principal of Ripon College Cuddesdon and the Oxford Ministry Course. Since 2004 he has also been Professor of Theological Education at King's College London, and Canon Theologian of Sheffield Cathedral. He is also the Chair of Cuddesdon and Denton Parish Council, and serves as an Associate Priest in the local 'Team Cluster' of Cuddesdon, Horspath and Garsington.

Anne Richards is National Adviser on mission theology, alternative spiritualities and new religious movements in the Mission and Public Affairs Division of the Archbishops' Council. She is a member of the Church of England's Rural Strategy Group and a prolific author and writer.

Mark Sanders is Diocesan Director of Ordinands and New Ministers in the Diocese of St Edmundsbury and Ipswich. He was born in the West Midlands, but began his ministry in a Suffolk team that included the fascinating mix of London overspill town and small rural villages. An incumbency in a suburban village followed. He works in many rural benefices and with many rural ministers.

Trevor Willmott has been Bishop of Basingstoke since 2002, prior to which he was Archdeacon of Durham. A major theme of his ministry has been the discernment, training and deployment of the church's ministers. Now in Winchester diocese, he is much engaged in helping the local church to reshape itself for mission. He is deeply committed to issues of justice and, in particular, the church's responsibility and response to those who are in prison. He is also much engaged in the field of ecumenism.

Dagmar Winter is the Rural Affairs Officer for the Diocese of Newcastle and Priest-in-Charge of Kirkwhelpington with Kirkharle, Kirkheaton and Cambo. She is a member of General Synod of the Church of England and its Rural Strategy Group, Vice-Chair of the North East Rural Affairs Forum, and Chaplain to Farm Crisis Network in Northumberland. Prior to her current post she was Associate Vicar at Hexham Abbey and Deanery Training Officer in a deanery that straddled the borders of Northumberland and Cumbria. She has a doctorate in theology on the Historical Jesus from the University of Heidelberg.

Acknowledgements

We are particularly grateful to the eight authors who contributed their knowledge and insight to the challenging area of rural mission and ministry and who responded with grace to the editorial process. Our thanks go also to the Rural Bishops' Panel of the House of Bishops of the Church of England, and to those many others who have supported our work.

We offer our thanks to the participants in the colloquium in April 2008 and who made a significant contribution to the shaping of this work: the Revd Dr Malcolm Brown, the Revd Stephen Cope, Helen Dobson, Geoff Dodgson, Prebendary Graham Earney, the Rt Revd Michael Langrish, the Revd Dr Georgina Morley, the Revd Jim Mynors, the Revd Philip Richter, Canon Mark Rylands, Stephen Rymer, the Rt Revd Alan Smith, the Prebendary Mrs Diana Taylor, the Revd Philip Wagstaff, and the Revd Dr David Way.

Introduction

The chapters in this collection originate from the work of the Rural Bishops' Panel. The issues discussed are clearly common to the whole church, albeit experienced differently in various contexts: how to be church in a period of rapid change; how to be faithful to God in engagement with the life and issues of the world; how to resource those called to specific ministries in the life of the local church. These are the themes that have guided this work, and are critical to the life and witness of the church that is, in the wording of the Church of England's Declaration of Assent, called 'to proclaim the faith afresh in every generation'. But in our judgement these themes have particular resonance within the rural context. The dialogue between implicit and explicit understandings of faith and discipleship; the need and desire to raise the awareness of vocation to a whole range of ministries; the value of building and place; the nature and exercise of leadership are all on the agenda of the rural church.

The challenge of the rural church therefore is both to itself, the rural church in its many-faceted contexts, and to the whole church – urban, suburban and rural.

We hope that this work will continue to stir up that necessary conversation with scripture, tradition, and the living witness of the church, which enables us all to grow personally and corporately in the discipleship of Jesus Christ. While the chapters are placed in a particular order – moving from reflection on context through the ministry of the whole people of God towards the calling and support of specific ministries – each one can be considered separately. At the end of each chapter are questions for reflection and discussion in small groups, such as a home group or deanery chapter.

This book is intended to stimulate, refresh and strengthen those who are already working in rural areas and encourage and enable those considering rural ministry. The rural church offers many opportunities for the future.

+James Bell, +Trevor Willmott, Jill Hopkinson
2009

I

Reading the context

JAMES BELL, JILL HOPKINSON, TREVOR WILLMOTT

See, consider, watch, look.[1] With these words, Jesus regularly invited his followers to pay attention to what was happening around them, observing the features of their context and reflecting on what they and God were about.

This introductory chapter looks at the rural context under three broad headings: social, economic and environment. Through these, it discusses the realities that need our attention as we respond to the calling to participate in the *missio Dei*: the sharing and showing and telling of the overflowing, reconciling, sacrificial love of God.

This participation in the *missio Dei* is one of the key themes in the *Mission-shaped Church* report and its successor books.[2] The idea of a mission-shaped church suggests the question of what 'shape' the rural church needs to have in order to share most fruitfully in the mission of God for his world. Our argument is that it needs first and foremost to be shaped for attention: watching out for where God is at work. As Rowan Williams has consistently reminded us, mission is 'finding out what God is doing and joining in'. The work of watching and listening is closely bound up in the scriptures with the idea of waiting for God, waiting on God. Before we share in God's mission, and as we do so, we need to be waiting on God, watching for God. Alan Roxborough has suggested that the missional leader's business is the cultivation of an environment that releases the missional imagination of God's people.[3] He goes on to say that:

At its core, [the] missional church is how we cultivate a congregational environment where God is the centre of conversation and God shapes the focus and work of the people. We
believe this is a shift in imagination for most congregations;
it is a change in the culture of congregational life. Missional
leadership is about shaping cultural imagination within a
congregation wherein people discern what God might be
about among them and in their community.[4]

Commenting helpfully on this change of culture, Alan
Roxborough also adds:

Culture change happens in a congregation when God's people
shift their attention to elements such as listening to Scripture;
dialoguing with one another; learning to listen; and becoming aware of and understanding what is happening in their
neighbourhood, community, and the places of their everyday lives. Instead of seeing these places and relationships as
potential for church growth, they come to be seen as places
where God's Spirit is present and calling us to enter with listening love. This shift sees God at work in one's context and
seeks to name what God might be up to. It is about seeing
the church in, with, and among the people and place where
we live, rather than in a specific building with a certain kind
of people.[5]

This surely is a very apt, if in some respects challenging, perspective for the rural church. A classic example would be ordained
and lay people engaging with the village school, whether a
church school or not, in order to meet and listen to all the
people, young and old, associated with it. From that meeting
and listening would come the ideas of how the church might
serve the members of the school community and how they saw
themselves participating in the life of the church.

Giving attention to the activity of God must include paying
attention to the Gospels, for being mission-shaped will always
mean being Christ-shaped. We read the Gospels to redis-

cover not only the content, but also the processes of Christian mission. Luke 10 would be a good example. Here Christ sends out the disciples in pairs to every place that he himself was going to visit, telling them that where they found themselves welcome they were to 'eat what is set before you, cure the sick who are there, and say to them, "the kingdom of God has come near to you"'.[6]

The story first suggests that partnership, one with another and together with Christ, is part of being and bringing the good news. Christ's directions indicate that we share good news first by receiving the hospitality of the world, then by demonstrating the closeness of the kingdom in appropriate ways, and finally by telling people what it all means. This pattern offers a fine working together of what is often held in contradistinction in terms of 'implicit' and 'explicit' mission. The distinction between implicit and explicit mission drawn by some could be characterized as being between presence and proclamation. Being present and welcoming and neighbourly would be seen as characteristics of the implicit model. Belonging would thus take priority over believing. In the explicit model, believing would take priority over belonging. A confession of personal faith would be the desired response to the declaration of the gospel, and that faith would be the basis of membership of the church.

In our view, implying that this must be a hard distinction between two opposing poles is not helpful when looking at the mission of the rural church. In the rural context, the anonymity characteristic of suburban and much urban living has not yet become the norm. Relationships and a sense of community are often highly cherished and therefore create the conditions for mission. The Luke 10 passage begins by recognizing that mission arises from *relationship* with Christ and in *being received* by the community. In this example, without relationship with Christ and reception by the community, mission cannot happen. Luke 10 suggests a further important principle for Christian mission: that for the sake of its integrity, faithful presence and appropriate action should precede words. Let us not talk of the rule of God before we have demonstrated it. Word and action are integrally bound up in the ministry of Jesus.

Giving attention to the Gospels requires hard work, ideally by the whole of the congregation. Alan Roxborough suggests the practice of focusing on a passage of the Gospels for several months to enable that Christ-shaping of the church to take place.[7] Clearly, prayer and careful thought would need to be given to the choice of passage and the structure for regular reflection on it. The community needs to ask how the passage might inform its understanding of what it is to be church and what steps might be necessary in order for it to enter more fully into that calling.

Within the Gospel accounts, we find that Christ himself paid the closest attention to his surroundings, both in noticing the people and the places, and how they lived. Hence his use of everyday events and occurrences, predominantly drawn from rural settings and circumstances, as the material for his parables. He also issues an invitation to his followers to notice, observe, watch and consider. If we take the incarnation seriously, we must also take the context seriously. Rowan Williams has written of paying 'real and costly attention to the real questions and the real agenda of those with whom we want to share the Good News'.[8] Reading the context as a participant in rural life rather than as an observer or visitor is to discover who and what needs to be addressed by the love of God and the message of the kingdom, and how that message might best be delivered. In other words, reading the context is the indispensable prerequisite of discovering the local church's vocation. It is essential that mission-shaped ministry is not exercised on the basis of the *assumed* reality but on the *actual* reality.

What is rural?

The areas around large towns and cities are characterized by open spaces and smaller communities. The countryside can occupy a sometimes mythical place in the collective psyche, illustrated in the paintings of Constable and Reynolds and by poets such as Tennyson. A beautiful landscape, with unchanging villages and hamlets, a few bucolic farmers. A place where nothing much happens and communities are close-knit and united. This rural idyll has never existed, and yet much of our understanding of rural is still influenced by these myths.

Rural areas have been defined by several different measures in recent years, some of which have been descriptive and others based on various maximum and minimum settlement sizes. Since 2004 the Department of the Environment, Food and Rural Affairs (Defra) has defined rural England based on population size and morphology (number of households within a 30-kilometre radius). Rural England is defined by two main categories: less sparse and sparse areas of population.[9] Most of rural England is less sparsely populated and reflects the relatively accessible areas surrounding large towns and cities. However, small areas of Somerset, Devon, Cornwall, Herefordshire, Shropshire, Cumbria, Yorkshire, Northumberland, Lincolnshire and Norfolk are sparsely populated. Unsurprisingly, these are generally the more remote parts of England, furthest from cities and major centres of employment.

A settlement is considered to be rural if it has a population of fewer than 10,000 people. This figure includes many market towns and reflects their importance for the life and economy of rural areas. There are three types of rural settlement used in the Defra definition: hamlets and isolated dwellings; villages; town and fringe.

Using this definition, people living in rural areas comprise 19.3% of the population of England, or 9.6 million people. Around half live in small towns, and only 3.1% live in settlements smaller than villages. Sparse rural areas contain only 1.4% of the population of England, around 723,000 people.[10] Sparsely populated areas have their own problems, with higher levels of deprivation and unemployment than less sparsely populated rural areas.

This definition, which is essentially quantitative in nature, does not acknowledge the social, economic or environmental aspects of rural areas.

Social realities

Rural communities have seen substantial demographic change in recent years, which has been driven in part by issues of an ageing population, increasing house prices, and the dispersed nature of deprivation in rural areas.

Demographic change

Rural populations are most concentrated around major urban centres, reflecting the intricate relationship between urban and rural life. The population of rural England has risen steadily over the last 20 years, with continuing net inward migration from towns and cities. The rural population has been growing faster in percentage terms than in urban areas, and between 1985 and 2005 the rural population grew by 13.7% (almost four times the rate of urban areas). Around 80,000 people move from towns and cities to the English countryside each year, with villages and hamlets in the less sparse areas experiencing the fastest growth. The majority of in-migrants are not people retiring to the countryside, but those aged between 30 and 50. Families (often with young children), seeking an improved life-style, are attracted by lower crime rates, a healthier environment, better schools and more attractive surroundings. For them, rural living is a lifestyle choice that they can afford.

However, there is significant out-migration of those aged between 15 and 24 as they move into higher education, seek employment, and try to find affordable housing. In 1985, rural and urban areas had age structures that were broadly similar, but 20 years on the proportion of the population aged between 15 and 29 had fallen from 21% to 15%.[11] It is expected that, as in-migrant adults age in situ, the age profile in the countryside, as a proportion of the population, will increase more significantly than that of the urban population. Rural England already has an ageing population, with around 2.3 million people aged over 60. Many of the oldest rural residents live in remote, sparsely populated areas, where the services they need are more difficult for both statutory and voluntary agencies to provide.

Migrant workers

Migrant workers are an important part of modern rural life, contributing to the agricultural and food processing industries (without whom much fresh produce would not be harvested), tourism, hospitality, construction and health care. Rural areas have experienced a significant growth in the number of migrant workers. 'The movement of migrant workers into many rural communities, principally from EU Accession countries, is having an increasingly significant impact on those host communities in terms of demands placed on education, training, housing and support services.'[12] The presence of migrant workers in an area may be perceived in a negative and divisive way, perhaps even resulting in racism; or be seen to enrich local life. In some cases the presence of these workers may be hidden, going unobserved by the local population, except on rare occasions. The recent economic uncertainty has already seen changes in the rate of migrant workers entering the UK, with initial indications being that numbers are declining. The impact of these changes on the agriculture, tourism and hospitality industries is as yet unknown.

The rural community

'beautifully set amidst glorious rolling countryside and approached off a long private driveway . . .'

'An impressive family house set in landscaped gardens in a sought after village . . .'

'Situated on the edge of a famous village bordering common land and enjoying far-reaching views . . .'

'A beautifully presented family home in this popular village . . .'

These quotations from estate agents' particulars perpetuate the myth of the rural idyll of well-known or popular villages – the ones that people will pay a premium to live in. What is less frequent in these descriptions of houses are descriptions of the local communities of which purchasers will become a part. At best, local schools and shops will be mentioned and perhaps the presence of a historic church building, but more attention will be given, particularly for the more expensive properties, as to whether the house has secluded grounds, private access or is in open countryside.

For some rural residents, identity can be experienced in terms of place and community. For others, especially those in the hinterlands of major cities, the village acts purely as dormitory or a place for recreation. Those whose networks of relationships may be elsewhere during the week often demonstrate little time or inclination to become involved in the wider life of the community.

The *Oxford English Dictionary* defines community as: 'a group of people living together in one place' and 'the people of an area or country considered collectively; society'. However, a community is more than just a group of people who all live in the same geographical location. As Michael Langrish puts it: 'people in "community" share something in common and, through sharing that something and being conscious that they do so, interact with one another in that context'.[13] However, '"community" is as difficult to define, as "communities" are difficult to identify and to promote'.[14]

A rural community, once thought of as a static geographical entity or 'the essence of the English good life – a collection of people well integrated into their local society and living productive and rewarding lives'[15] – is now more nuanced. Even in remote and sparsely populated areas the concept of commonality within a geographical area is less and less the case. Malcolm Moseley, quoting A. W. Rogers, defines community as: 'a collection of people in a given locality who share a common identity and who interact to form some sort of local social system'.[16] A rural community will now be made up of several (or many) different groups and networks of people. Among others, groups and networks will be associated with the local school, pub or shop, any sports clubs and remaining industry, the church or chapel, and older people's organizations. Many newer residents, though, will only have tenuous links to the place where they live, with networks of friends and families based elsewhere. Rural living is still a significant draw with people wishing to live in a place where they perceive there to be a greater level of good neighbourliness, safety and potential for personal interaction. However, social isolation is increasingly recognized as a problem for a growing number of rural residents. The communal idyll where everyone goes and gets involved is still perpetuated, though, contributing to the concept of community as a commodity to be bought into. While communality may still be present in some places, it has generally been replaced by communities where only a few people go to specific events associated with their own groups or networks. The village pub is a good example of this change. Once a meeting place for people from many different walks of life, in order to survive many pubs have now specialized in high-quality food in order to become more regional attractions.

Long-term residents are likely to come from a core group of village families who have lived there for generations – either local farmers and their workers or those employed in other local industries. Their housing today is unlikely to be in tied cottages or the older village houses, but in council-owned properties or newer houses on the edge of the village.[17] A large proportion of people who live in rural communities today are first-generation villagers who are most likely to be commuters and their families. The other main group is the retired, who may have moved to the village on retirement but are more likely to have lived there as commuters.

The presence of large numbers of new residents has seen communities change from a place of work to one that is purely residential. In some cases the countryside has become somewhat suburbanized, particularly where planning has allowed new developments in settlements to be separated from the existing housing, or created a series of 'closes' that go nowhere. Where new developments by their look, the closeness of building and proximity to main roads, preserve a suburban outlook, they also contribute to a feeling of separateness for newcomers to the village.

Belonging

Belonging has traditionally been thought of largely in terms of a rural settlement or place, but clearly now needs to be expressed in terms of different groups, organizations or networks. David Walker[18] offers one interpretative model of belonging that can be applied helpfully in rural areas, but will not necessarily apply in all situations.

The *established residents* are likely to have lived in the rural community for a long time, perhaps for many generations, and have a strong sense of belonging to that place. There are strong local ties, although these people may not play an active part in the community. *Commuters*, much more prevalent now, are individuals and family groups that commute out of the settlement for work – and increasingly for all aspects of their lives – and, as a result, often have little time and energy left to take part in local activities. Similar groups are *privacy seekers*, who want to escape from the city but remain deeply connected to it; and *trophy owners*, whose homes are symbols of success. Both these groups do not belong to the wider community, but rather to their homes and achievements.

Lifestyle shifters move to rural areas usually to be part of community life, often reflecting a long-held sense of belonging to a place, or the countryside in general. Some take part in local institutions as a way of developing a sense of belonging within a new community. Parents at home with children, the retired and home-workers are *full-time dwellers* and are more dependent on the facilities in the locality, especially schools. Older and less mobile residents may feel isolated; others may have time to engage in local activities and groups.

The *missing vulnerable* are people who have reached a crisis in their lives and are forced out of their local communities at times of greatest need. Local towns provide far more rented accommodation than villages, though, and most social housing provision is in towns. The *arriving vulnerable*, such as older people in ill health or lone parents, tend to be looking for networks of support and groups that they can be part of to help them belong to the community. *Travellers and gypsies* are often the most marginalized group in any community. Their distinctive lifestyle, reliance on seasonal work, and strong sense of belonging to their own community can easily be perceived as threatening and intrusive by others.

Absent friends are those who have a sense of belonging (and even ownership) of a place where they do not live because they have moved away or are descendants of existing or previous residents. To these people, the community has a sense of 'home' about it and they do not want it or the church to change. *Tourists and visitors* are those who have come to look at the village, visit its pub or to walk in the countryside, and they feel the village belongs to them for the time they are there. Finally, there is the *British public:* the countryside belongs to the whole nation and is used by individuals in different ways.

All of these groups will interact in differing ways with each other and the wider community, and they may be in tension or conflict.

Social capital and community cohesion

Social capital describes a wide variety of quite specific benefits that flow from the trust, reciprocity, information and co-operation associated with good social networks. Or, as Robert Putnam puts it, 'features of social organisation, such as networks, norms, and trust that facilitate coordination and cooperation for mutual benefit'.[19]

Social capital is therefore social engagement that gives people access to support, opportunities and information which enables them to pursue their own goals and achieve well-being. It can foster trust and build a community's capacity to further organize and prosper. There are three different types of social capital in common use: bonding, bridging and linking.

Bonding social capital is the strong relationships and networks formed within communities by friendships between neighbours and through groups such as the Women's Institute, sports clubs or the church congregation. It can also be negative, forming exclusive groups that others find intimidating or difficult to join. *Bridging* social capital reflects the networks that form across social groups and communities. This is also shown through the multiple groups one person might be a member of within a rural community or, more importantly, hold responsibility within. *Linking* social capital is the networks and connections between communities and external institutions. Linking social capital tends to represent connections that are made outside the immediate locality of the community to external organizations such as district councils, charitable organizations and, importantly, to other communities. Whether they are in the immediate locality, or are national or even international, they can bring benefit to that community.

Social capital is generally a positive force within rural communities and one that holds communities together, whether it is through informal relationships or formal groups and organizations. However, isolation affects all age ranges in rural areas, particularly older people and those living and working in remote places. Rural organizations, shops and pubs – and especially rural churches – play a significant part in contributing to the relationships of knowing and being known that hold a community together. These relationships can be challenged by those who live in the community but do not want to take part in it – such as some second-home owners, commuters who lead separate lives, and those who seek privacy. The opportunities to meet and form relationships are also compromised by the removal of public services such as the post office, shop, pub, church and school, which all act as a place for social interaction and casual encounter. The interlocking relationships of different groups and networks can also be fragmented by a decline in volunteering which, for example, leads to the closure of sports clubs and activities for young people.

Village schools, particularly primary schools, make a significant and important contribution to social capital in rural communities, often becoming an essential focus. There are 4,470 Church of England primary schools (25.3% of the total number); just over half of these are in rural areas and 38.4% of all pupils are in rural schools.[20] This is a lasting and essential contribution to rural communities and their futures. Schools help to create links between families with children and all aspects of village life, and especially with the older generation. Families with children are often committed to activities taking place in the school as well as the wider community, normally to everyone's benefit. The school gate is also an important point for communication, creating an informal hub for news and opportunities for the building of social capital, both bonding and bridging. These relationships are broken or become fragmented if the school is closed. However, the much vaunted government presumption against closure of rural schools has been challenged in some predominantly rural counties. In many places rural schools are under the threat of closure, sometimes for reasons of quality or extremely small size. Increasingly, with tighter local authority budgets, expediency will play a bigger role, threatening the social cohesion of those communities.

The withdrawal or closure of facilities such as schools or pubs, and the negative impact this has on social interaction, raises issues of cohesion and fragmentation within rural communities. Cohesion and fragmentation are complex issues that equally apply to rural areas. All communities have their tensions, and in rural communities these may well be around issues such as a lack of provision for young people, limited or non-existent public transport, tensions between long-term residents and newcomers such as commuters, second-home owners and migrant workers. Affluence and social deprivation are also factors. In rural communities it is possible for different groups and networks to live entirely parallel lives within the same settlement.

Rural church

There are at least 13,000 churches of all denominations present in rural areas of England. The Church of England has a presence in almost every community, through the parish system. Of 16,000 Anglican churches in 13,000 parishes in England, 9,639 churches are rural, 60% of the total. Approximately 40% of the electoral roll of the Church of England is from a rural church.[21] Overall, around 13,000 churches are listed, and churches are often the oldest buildings still in use in the settlement.[22]

Almost every rural parish has to share its priest with one or more parishes. In some parts of the country it is not uncommon to have very large numbers of parishes grouped together into multi-parish benefices or team ministries. Commonly, multi-parish benefices comprise three to nine parishes, but the numbers can be as high as 20 for team ministries, although this is rare. Since the 1970s there has been a significant transfer of personnel and resources from the rural to the urban church and, as a result, many parishes have been subject to pastoral reorganization on several occasions over the last 40 years.

The creation of a multi-parish benefice, where the priest has cure of souls of more than one parish, is a significant feature of rural church life. It brings with it a high level of complexity and the burden of multiple systems and responsibilities. This is reflected in the service rota, meetings of PCCs, several buildings to maintain, and several communities to get to know and in which to build relationships with other organizations. While groups of parishes working together offer the potential for variety and creating critical mass for activities over a wider area, the governance of these structures, and the role of and expectations placed upon the priest, are difficult and challenging. Old models of ministry now have to be replaced by collaboration and oversight.

At the end of 2007 there were 20,355 licensed ministers, both clergy and readers, working in the Church of England. Of these, 10,000 are readers. In addition, there were 7,000 retired clergy with permission to officiate and 1,600 chaplains to prisons, hospitals and education.[23] In recent years the numbers of people offering themselves for non-stipendiary (or self-supporting) ministry has grown significantly. This also includes ordained local ministers in some dioceses. Non-stipendiary ministers (NSMs) make an essential contribution to mission and ministry in rural areas and are increasing in number, being appointed as priest-in-charge of rural multi-parish benefices. Alan Smith estimates there to be at least 3,000 NSMs working in the Church of England today.[24]

Rural church and social capital

Rural churches have an important role to play in offering opportunities for service, worship and social events to bring communities together, thereby contributing to both bonding and bridging social capital. The informal and formal activities of congregation members – such as visiting, providing practical support, and being a member of a village organization (including the church) – are important bonding activities, and it should be noted that the informal activities of congregation members make as much contribution to social capital as formal organizations and events.[25] Bridging social capital can be created through events and festivals, links with schools, and by making use of community meeting spaces, for example. This allows networks to overlap and develops relationships between different groups and generations.

Richard Farnell and colleagues[26] identified some key functions of churches in rural communities in the creation of social capital:

- Rural churches can act as a place for barriers to be broken down between different social groups, allowing people to meet on equal terms.
- The organization of social activities was valued and felt to be important by the wider community, as were special services and events.

- Members of rural congregations volunteered to lead and organize a wide range of other community organizations and events.
- Church ministers also play an important part in terms of community leadership and influence.
- Partnership working, the sharing of expertise and resources were essential contributors to the social capital generated by churches.

In addition, congregation members are also able to develop linking social capital by forming relationships with groups and organizations outside the immediate rural community that bring wider benefits both to the church and community.

As a result of the creation of bonding, bridging and linking social capital through deep involvement in community life, no barriers were perceived between church and community life, and the two were thought to be synonymous. Many 'identified their faith as being an important and distinctive driver of voluntary action and as underpinning a sense of shared identity'.[27]

Economic realities

It is now important to describe rural economies, not just economy, reflecting the diversity of situations in which economic activity takes place within rural England.[28] In the ten years to 2005, rural areas experienced a faster rate of economic growth than large urban areas, especially in the 'knowledge intensive sector'.[29] This also reflects the change from a unified and traditionally based agrarian economy to one that embraces innovation and technology. Businesses in rural areas registered for VAT/PAYE earned £321 billion in 2006 (10% of the turnover of English firms); and 11% of people are self-employed in rural areas, a greater proportion than urban, which may represent an enterprising community or an absence of alternative opportunities.

The public service sector (28%) and distribution, hotels, catering and repairs (21%) are the largest employers in both rural and urban areas. Unemployment rates tend to be lower in rural areas, with 4% of the working age population unemployed. But there are important local variations, with some areas having very low rates or very high rates of unemployment. Sparse rural areas and peripheral rural districts remain among the least prosperous economies in England. By contrast, less sparse areas are able to compete with major urban areas in terms of productivity, new business registrations, growth and employment.[30]

The total income from UK farming was £2.5 billion in 2007, rising to £5.7 billion on a value added basis.[31] However, individual farm incomes depend upon the enterprise type, with the livestock sector particularly subject to variable and unpredictable prices. The cost of fertilizers, pesticides and other inputs continues to fluctuate with the variable cost of oil. The numbers employed in agriculture have continued to decline to 353,000 in 2007, or less than 2% of the national workforce.[32] However, the countryside is an essential part of the tourism industry, which in turn provides the single largest contribution, by both employment and income, to the rural economy. In 2007 Visit Britain estimated that rural tourism generated £14 billion in income and supported 380,000 jobs (both full and part time).[33] Churches are also an important part of tourism in rural areas, attracting people to places that they might not otherwise visit.

The impact of the recession, which started in 2008, will have a particularly negative effect on those who are already disadvantaged and rely on seasonal or temporary work for most of their income. The impact on rural communities could be quite considerable, particularly through the further loss of shops, pubs and other local services as well as businesses based in rural areas. It is as yet unclear how many additional people will be facing unemployment in rural areas, particularly among people who have commuted to work in large towns and cities. As a result, the absence of public transport in many places will become a more serious problem as people struggle to find new sources of work and access benefits, advice and support.

Advantage and disadvantage

Rural communities are commonly perceived as being affluent, and for the most part this is true. In general, average household incomes are higher in rural areas as large numbers of people commute from hamlets and villages to well-paid jobs in nearby towns and cities. As a result, standards of living are high and rural areas are still seen as a good and safe place to live. However, the average figures mask the differences within rural areas. Sparse areas particularly, with their distance from major cities or peripheral locations, have much lower household incomes – in some cases lower than in some urban areas.

There are significant levels of poverty in rural areas, often exacerbated by the differential between neighbours, isolation and absence of alternatives (for example, in employment). Poverty in rural areas is also largely hidden. In a place where you are known, even if not by everyone, it is almost impossible to admit that there is a problem.

In large towns and cities poverty may be concentrated in easily identified deprived areas. In rural areas, disadvantage is dispersed. The Index of Multiple Deprivation (IMD) is used to identify areas of poverty, but it is not sensitive enough to pick up the individual deprived households or small groups of households who are deprived in rural areas. For example, only 2.4% of the 20% most deprived areas by the IMD are rural (calculated by Lower Super Output Areas of 1,500 people), but 15% of all deprived people are rural residents.[34] Where the IMD does identify rural areas that are significantly disadvantaged, these tend to be both sparsely populated and remote, or ex-industrial or ex-mining communities, and are deprived in terms of household income, employment opportunities and education. The greater the distance from urban centres, the lower the income from employment. This is particularly true for rural coastal communities.

The Commission for Rural Communities has calculated that 906,101 households are in income poverty in rural areas.[35] This means that just over one-fifth of all rural households in

England have an income of less than £16,800 per annum. This is estimated to be around 2 million people dispersed across the whole of England and will include a large number of children and young people.

The Commission for Rural Communities has identified three critical factors for rural people, in both experiencing and escaping disadvantage:

1 Financial poverty – income and employment.
2 Access poverty – accessing transport and other services.
3 Network poverty – contact and help from friends, neighbours and others.

Financial poverty is reflected not just in lower incomes or small pensions, but also in reduced uptake of benefits, as rural residents are less likely to claim the benefits to which they are entitled.[36] Jobs in rural areas are characterized by limited choice, can be seasonal or temporary in nature, and tend to be lower paid than equivalent jobs in urban areas.

Transport plays an essential role in allowing people to access all the necessary things in life, such as education, health care, shopping and employment. Despite high levels of car ownership in rural areas, one-third of adults do not have access to a car. Therefore providing suitable public or alternative means of transport is essential for this group of people. However, there is also a need to retain or provide services at the most local level to overcome the need for people to travel. Information technology also has an important role in alleviating access poverty.

For people who are in poverty there may be a fear of being identified, and of their private business being known to others. Where communities have become fragmented or families have moved away, those who are disadvantaged are likely to be isolated and have limited choices for even the most basic needs in life. Social isolation and an absence of friendship and support lead to disadvantage, increased ill health and poverty in rural areas. The perception of a strong rural community life remains, but it is usually the disadvantaged who are excluded from this. Without strong networks of family and friends giving the benefits of social interaction, gains (such as better mental health) are lost. Retaining local services such as shops and post offices and the activities associated with community groups, community halls and the church, all assist in providing venues and opportunities for social interaction that can help in avoiding or overcoming network poverty and social isolation.

Housing

House prices in rural areas have seen the highest rises and consistent growth in the most recent boom period. Property in less sparsely populated, more easily accessible hamlets was sold for the highest prices. The ratio between house price and household income is a helpful guide to affordability. The higher the ratio, the less affordable a property. Housing affordability is 9.0 in less sparse villages and hamlets, but higher still at 9.7 for sparse rural areas, reflecting the lower incomes of households in these locations.[37]

The absence of affordable housing for a great many people and families is having a significant impact on the make-up of rural communities. It forces young people to live in nearby or even distant towns, some of whom may return to the village to work locally. It puts pressure on local services, particularly schools, as smaller numbers of children live in the area, reducing the school role to a potentially unviable number. Pressure is also felt by health and social service providers as the in situ population age and require a higher level of services.

Environmental realities

Place

The countryside is shaped by many different historical, geographical, environmental, economic and social factors.

The current layout of a village is likely to have been shaped by the history of many centuries. The Romans, the Vikings, the Norman invasion, the Black Death, the Civil War and local conflicts, and more latterly the Enclosure Act, along with industry, mining and extraction, forestry and agriculture, may all have contributed to the shape of the community today. Communities often formed around a religious establishment, with the surrounding land being owned by the Abbey. After the Reformation, land was given to the Tudor gentry, creating the Lord of the Manor, the impact of which is still present today in the shape, form and allegiance of many communities. More latterly, the presence of a road, railway, canal or river may have meant that a settlement developed linearly, or offered a place of residence to those building, maintaining or reliant on them for trade. Nuclear-shaped settlements may historically have formed around a green, pond or, recently, a playing field. Settlements in the uplands may cluster houses on the hillside or string them out in the valley bottom.

Landscape on a larger scale informs not only the morphology of a place, but also its identity. Settlements in the uplands will have a very different look and feel to settlements in the open lowlands, the fens or on the coast. The history (and shape) of these different places will have been influenced by varying extremes of climate: storms and high winds, flooding or snowfall, high or low temperatures. Those places that have previously been reliant on either the land or the sea for their living for a substantial proportion of the population will still be informed and influenced by this relationship, even though it may now have little economic significance.

The shape and layout of these settlements will also have been affected by the nature and size of local employment. Ex-industrial villages will be by their very nature places where a significant number of people lived and worked, therefore having quite densely packed houses and streets. New developments may happen at the edge of a village, on the site of a redundant farm and its buildings, or as infill within the village. All these change the nature of that place for ever.

A settlement is also shaped by its proximity to other settlements such as a market town or a city. These larger places influence both the identity, and ultimately the morphology, of the smaller settlements adjacent to them. Villages closer to larger population and business centres often have a large number of newer houses whose residents commute to work elsewhere. Settlements that are close to good communication links such as main roads or the railway are also likely to have seen a significant amount of new housing in the last 30 years. Communities remote from transport or larger towns and cities tend to rely on local sources of employment and therefore exist in a very different way. However, they too may well have seen significant new building in the last three or four decades.

Social history is particularly important to an understanding of place. This is informed by the presence or absence of landowners who may either be benign or draconian (and the presence of any associated tied housing for estate workers). The Lord of the Manor may still own a large proportion of the housing. Prevailing occupations, style of building, village organizations and local businesses such as shops or pubs, are among many other factors that are important. This history may, over the years, have both united and divided residents and these fault lines may still be part of the collective consciousness of the long-term residents. To newer residents, learning these stories may be seen as part of belonging or sharing in the identity of that place – but they may also be seen as irrelevant to modern life.

Identity takes on a particularly important role in very small communities. By their very nature they may feel insular or threatened, and while this may lead to the development of a strong cohesive community, it may also contribute to the exclusion of newcomers or a reluctance to accept change.

Land use

Some 8.6% of the land area of England is in built-up settlements, although about half of this area is maintained as gardens and green space. The major urban areas of England cover 5.3% of land, around 0.8% is rural towns, and 1.0% is villages and hamlets. For the remaining land area, agriculture accounts for

70% and woodland and forestry a further 8%.[38] There is evidence that the countryside has accommodated proportionately more new-build houses since 1998 than urban areas.[39] Pressure for development in rural areas remains, particularly for affordable housing and, with limited brown-field sites and many disused buildings already converted, new building will inevitably take place on green fields.

Almost half the land in England under agricultural production is used for grazing livestock, and 40% for arable production. The landscape has been shaped by human activity and farming for thousands of years. Areas considered to be of particular importance are protected by inclusion in an Area of Outstanding Natural Beauty or in a National Park (among other designations). Much of the land within these areas is managed by those who farm it. Consistent reform of the Common Agricultural Policy has required that land used for farming is now multi-functional in nature. Not only is it used to grow and produce food, but to support wildlife habitats, biodiversity and other environmental goods.[40] Public goods are also required in the form of landscape protection, which is essential to maintain tourism in many rural areas. Farmers must comply with a series of regulations on animal health and welfare, environmental protection and waste control (known as cross-compliance) in order to receive a Single Farm Payment. Land under agricultural production is therefore subject to intense scrutiny.

Food prices had been declining across the world over a prolonged period, until the autumn of 2007 when prices rose steeply. This was related to drought and flooding in different parts of the world; the rising cost of oil and oil-based inputs such as fertilizers and pesticides; changing patterns of meat consumption in India and China; and the use of some crops for biofuel production. Biofuel production now competes with the growing of food on productive land – particularly in North America, but also in the UK. Since then, prices have fluctuated. The UK is around 60% self-sufficient in food and 74% self-sufficient in foods that can be produced in this country.[41]

Climate change

'Warming of the climate system is unequivocal, as is now evident from observations of increases in global average air and ocean temperatures, widespread melting of snow and ice and rising global average sea level.'[42] This quote from the International Panel on Climate Change (IPCC) sums up the challenges facing the international community. The UK and its rural areas will not be immune from the impact of these changes. Increases in temperature, changes to weather patterns with greater extremes of weather, longer and more severe droughts, stronger winds and higher levels of precipitation are already evident. The increase in greenhouse gas emissions through human activity, also known as 'anthropogenic' emissions, are 'very likely'[43] to have caused increases in global average temperatures. Emissions of carbon dioxide, methane and nitrous oxide have grown by 70% between 1970 and 2004.[44]

For Europe, the projected impacts include an increased risk of flooding both inland and coastal, with the potential for more erosion as a result. In mountainous areas there will be reduced snow cover in winter with glacier retreat and significant loss of species. There will be an increased risk of heat waves due to a consistent rise in temperature with associated drought and reduced crop yields.[45] Cooler lowland areas may well benefit from increased crop yields as a result of temperature rises.

In rural communities in England climate change is evident in an earlier spring, a longer growing season and extremes of weather, such as the wet summers of 2007 and 2008 and the associated severe flooding of July 2007. In the future, longer, drier summers will put significant pressure on water resources, particularly for irrigation of crops by abstraction from rivers, as well as increased demand for domestic use.

Although agriculture makes only a small contribution to carbon dioxide emissions (about 1% of total UK carbon emissions),[46] emissions of methane from livestock and organic wastes and nitrous oxides from soils are large – 23% of the

UK's methane production, and 63% of nitrous oxide production, is from agricultural sources. However, the amount of these gases emitted since 1990 has declined steadily.[47]

There is some evidence that human activity in rural areas results in a larger amount of carbon emissions per person than in urban areas.[48] This is mostly caused by a higher income and per capita consumption (based on size of dwelling and number of cars).[49] There are also greater emissions through heating (for hard-to-heat homes – for example, those that have solid walls) and because of the greater distances travelled by rural residents. Housing is the largest contributor to a domestic carbon footprint, followed by transport, consumer items and food. On this basis rural residents may find it particularly difficult to reduce the emissions associated with normal daily activities.

Reflecting on the local context

This chapter began by inviting the reader to see, consider, watch, look; to be aware of the complex factors that have shaped the context of the unique rural area in which they have an interest. Rural areas reveal these factors in powerful ways, and this is what makes our rural environment and its diverse communities so interesting and challenging. Yet, perhaps because so much of our media is generated in a metropolitan culture, and a great deal of national policy also seems to be framed around urban concerns, the complexities and rootedness of rural community life sometimes seems absent from images of public life, and even rural people themselves may lack the words and concepts to describe their own situation. All mission and all ministry ought to be contextual, but, just as the pressures on the inner cities in the 1980s led to an exciting explosion of contextual theology and new practices of urban mission, so today it may well be the rural areas that are most in danger of marginalization from national life. The pattern of rural marginalization will not be the same as the urban, nor will the contextual mission practices and theology be the same; but, as the Church of England gains a revived focus for mission, the need for contextual rural understandings of sharing Christian faith today is at the top of the agenda.

The way faith is expressed is also conditioned by the multi-layered context in which it is lived. Thus Cumbria is not Devon; Hampshire is not North Yorkshire – and even these generalizations will be challenged by a more local definition of identity. For those who lead local churches, understanding the context in which they are ministering is a fundamental requirement. 'And the Word became flesh and lived among us . . . full of grace and truth.'[50]

How, then, does the church-in-mission respond in such a way that its message and its values are best communicated?

Questions

How do scripture and tradition affect or influence the way(s) in which you seek to discern the mission of the church?

Social realities

- What does belonging mean in your community? How might the church contribute to the different forms of social capital?

- What activities take place in your rural community? Are they secure and widely owned, or struggling and precarious? What opportunities are there to celebrate their contribution to community life and to support those who run them?

Economic realities

- Which of David Walker's categories of belonging (pp. 10ff.) apply to your community?

- What are the working patterns of your area? How far are these patterns represented among church members, and how might the church relate to local economic activity?

- What are the issues of justice in your community for the young and for the disadvantaged? How might the church be an agent for change?

Environmental realities

- What are the main historical influences that have shaped the identity of your community? Which of these influences have continuing relevance today? What role has faith played in shaping the community and what roles might it have in the future?

- How is climate change likely to affect your community: now and in the future? In what ways are the issues of climate change on the agenda of your local community? How might the church in your area act as an example of environmental responsibility?

Notes

1 Luke 12.54–56; Luke 12.24; Mark 12.41; John 4.35.

2 *Mission-shaped Church*, London: Church House Publishing, 2002. See also the *Mission-shaped* series from Church House Publishing: *Mission-shaped Parish*; *Mission-shaped and Rural*; *Mission-shaped Spirituality*.

3 Alan J. Roxborough and Fred Romanuk, *The Missional Leader: Equipping Your Church to Reach a Changing World*, San Francisco: Jossey-Bass, 2006.

4 Roxborough and Romanuk, *Missional Leader*, p. 26.

5 Roxborough and Romanuk, *Missional Leader*, pp. 63–4.

6 Luke 10.8–9.

7 Roxborough and Romanuk, *Missional Leader*, p. 43.

8 'Mixed economy', *Journal of Fresh Expressions*, 2008, http://www.freshexpressions.org.uk/mixedeconomy (accessed 20 April 2009).

9 Department of the Environment, Food and Rural Affairs, *Rural Strategy 2004*, London: Department of the Environment, Food and Rural Affairs, 2004.

10 Commission for Rural Communities, *State of the Countryside 2008*, Wetherby: Commission for Rural Communities Publications, 2008.

11 Commission for Rural Communities, *State of the Countryside*

2007, Wetherby: Commission for Rural Communities Publications, 2007, p. 14.

12 Commission for Rural Communities, *State of the Countryside 2007*, p. 18.

13 Michael L. Langrish, 'Dynamics of community', in Jeremy Martineau, Leslie J. Francis and Peter Francis (eds), *Changing Rural Life: A Christian Response to Key Rural Issues*, Norwich: Canterbury Press, 2004, p. 22.

14 Malcolm J. Moseley, *Rural Development: Principles and Practice*, London: Sage Publications, 2003, p. 73.

15 A. W. Rogers, *English Rural Communities: An Assessment and Prospects for the 1990s*, Salisbury: Rural Development Commission, 1993, pp. 20–1, quoted in Langrish, 'Dynamics of community', p. 22.

16 Rogers, *English Rural Communities*, p. 5, quoted in Moseley, *Rural Development*, p. 74.

17 Timothy Jenkins, *Religion in English Everyday Life: An Ethnographic Approach*, Oxford: Berghahn Books, 1999, pp. 50–1.

18 David S. Walker, 'Belonging to rural church and society: theological and sociological perspectives', *Rural Theology*, 4(2), Issue 67, 2006, pp. 85–97.

19 Robert D. Putnam, 'The prosperous community: social capital and public life', *The American Prospect*, vol. 4, no. 13, 1993, http://www.prospect.org/cs/articles?article=the_prosperous_community (accessed 20 April 2009).

20 Estimate by the Church of England Education Division, March 2009.

21 Figures calculated by the Research and Statistics Division of the Archbishops' Council.

22 http://www.cofe.anglican.org/about/builtheritage/ (accessed 20 April 2009).

23 http://www.cofe.anglican.org/about/thechurchofenglandtoday (accessed 20 April 2009).

24 Alan Smith, *God-shaped Mission*, Norwich: Canterbury Press, 2008, p. 18.

25 J. Flint, R. Atkinson and A. Kearns, *Churches and Social Capital: The Role of Church of Scotland Congregations in Local Community Development*, University of Glasgow, 2002.

26 R. Farnell, J. Hopkinson, D. Jarvis, J. Martineau and J. Ricketts Hein, *Faith in Rural Communities: Contributions of Social Capital to Community Vibrancy*, Stoneleigh Park: Acora Publishing, 2006.

27 Jemma Grieve, Veronique Jochum, Belinda Pratten and Claire Steel, *Faith in the Community: The Contribution of Faith-based Organisations to Rural Voluntary Action*, London: NCVO, 2007, p. 25.

28 Commission for Rural Communities, *England's Rural Areas:*

Steps to Release Their Economic Potential – Advice from the Rural Advocate to the Prime Minister, Wetherby: Commission for Rural Communities Publications, 2008, p. 11.

29 Commission for Rural Communities, *State of the Countryside 2008*, pp. 99–101.

30 Commission for Rural Communities, *State of the Countryside 2008*, pp. 88ff.

31 Department of the Environment, Food and Rural Affairs (Defra), *Agriculture and Food – Quick Statistics*, 2008, https://statistics.defra.gov.uk/esg/quick/agri.asp (accessed 20 April 2009).

32 Commission for Rural Communities, *State of the Countryside 2008*, p. 100.

33 Visit Britain – personal communication.

34 Tom Smith, Stefan Noble and Julia Heynat, 'Measuring Rural Deprivation in England – Quantitative Analysis and Socio-economic Classification', Oxford Consultants for Social Inclusion. Presentation made at Commission for Rural Communities and Department of Communities and Local Government seminar on Measuring rural deprivation in England, 5 December 2008, http://www.ruralcommunities.gov.uk/publications/measuringruraldeprivationinruralenglandpresentationbyocsitocrcandclgseminar (accessed 20 April 2009).

35 Commission for Rural Communities, *State of the Countryside 2008*, pp. 77–8.

36 Commission for Rural Communities, *Rural Disadvantage Priorities for Action*, Wetherby: Commission for Rural Communities Publications, 2006, p. 11.

37 Commission for Rural Communities, *State of the Countryside 2008*, p. 42.

38 Commission for Rural Communities, *State of the Countryside 2008*, p. 114.

39 'Countryside quality counts' (2006), quoted in *State of the Countryside 2008*, p. 115.

40 This can be supported financially through the Entry Level Stewardship Scheme and other support schemes. For more information, see http://www.defra.gov.uk.

41 Department of the Environment, Food and Rural Affairs, *Ensuring the UK's Food Security in a Changing World*, London: Department of the Environment, Food and Rural Affairs, 2008, p. 16, http://www.defra.gov.uk/foodrin/policy/pdf/Ensuring-UK-Food-Security-in-a-changing-world-170708.pdf (accessed 24 April 2009).

42 International Panel on Climate Change, *Climate Change 2007: Synthesis Report. Summary for Policy Makers [of Fourth Assessment Report AR4]*, p. 2, http://www.ipcc.ch/pdf/assessment-report/ar4/syr/ar4_syr_spm.pdf (accessed 24 April 2009).

43 International Panel on Climate Change, *Climate Change 2007: Synthesis Report*, p. 5.

44 International Panel on Climate Change, *Climate Change 2007: Synthesis Report*, p. 5.

45 International Panel on Climate Change, *Climate Change 2007: Synthesis Report*, p. 11.

46 Commission for Rural Communities, *State of the Countryside 2008*, p. 146.

47 Commission for Rural Communities, *State of the Countryside 2008*, p. 146.

48 Commission for Rural Communities, *State of the Countryside 2007*, pp. 138–9.

49 Commission for Rural Communities, *State of the Countryside 2008*, pp. 144–5, 151.

50 John 1.14.

2

Distinctive features and values

JEREMY MARTINEAU

Introduction

The rural church has a central part in the past, present and future story of rural areas, and this chapter examines its key features and values through the characteristics and contribution of its people.

First it is necessary to be clear that the word 'church' is used to describe both the building and the people who use it. The rural church relates to its context more firmly than in urban areas as the church building serves several, sometimes subtle, purposes. It is a focus for the history of the community, providing continuity in that story. It is a totem around which life's key moments are celebrated. As frequently the most prominent structure, it gives a visual focus to many properties around, and identity to the community. In its grounds burials take place, making it a sacred space for many. It may increasingly be a well-used public space for secular and social activities, as well as religious ceremonies. It is a place of quiet and of peace used by individuals who may not attend public worship. The local school may also use the church for a range of activities. Most of all, it is the place where God is worshipped regularly. Thus the building is much valued, even by those who are not regular members of the congregation.

The rural community is blessed to be set in a natural landscape, one that is also the result of centuries of human endeavour. The church is often found at the centre of these communities. While not every rural settlement has a strong contemporary agricultural purpose, the surrounding country-side is valued by residents for its space, beauty, colour and a pleasant horizon.

Although 'church' is, in the public mind, a building, it is primarily the people who use that building – both for worship and as a focus for their spiritual journey – that define it. The key features of the rural church to be explored here are:

- The mercurial overlap between church and the local community.
- The issue of small-sized congregations.
- The way churches are linked together in increasing numbers and over a larger area under the care of one or more priests.
- The significance of worship.
- The role of the church building itself.

The chapter ends with suggestions about the special values that undergird the work of the church in rural areas.

The rural church and the local community

This section explores the linkage between the church and the local community. It asserts the importance of using the links and networks that are available through church members as local residents; working in partnership with other agencies is shown to be a positive way of engaging in mission.

False memories haunt the rural church. The first false memory is that churches were always full, and second, that parishes always had a resident vicar. In reality, clergy were normally shared between two or three parishes. While the Sunday activities of today have changed somewhat in the last 130 years, the numbers attending church are perhaps surprisingly familiar. It was not uncommon for churches to be built with a seating capacity that greatly exceeded the number of the local population. In her elegant memoir *Lark Rise to Candleford*, Flora Thompson describes church-going in a hamlet in east Oxfordshire in the 1880s:

If the Lark Rise people had been asked their religion, the answer of nine out of ten would have been 'Church of England', for practically all of them were christened, married and buried as such, although, in adult life, few went to church between the baptisms of their offspring. The children were shepherded there after Sunday school and about a dozen of their elders attended regularly; the rest stayed at home, the women cooking and nursing, and the men, after an elaborate Sunday toilet, . . . spent the rest of the day eating, sleeping, reading the newspaper, and strolling round to see how their neighbours' pigs and gardens were looking.[1]

The glory of the Anglican tradition in Britain is that the church at the local level is both a community in itself and also a key part of the wider community of residents, and such duality provides a missionary challenge. Support by residents for the parish church may bring with it a hope in the mind of the congregation of a more explicit commitment to Christian beliefs. The proper wish among clergy to see a more clearly stated commitment to the Christian faith challenges people to make up their mind about belief. The days of comfortable ambiguity are passing.

Those who are faithful to Christ's call also belong to a community of work, leisure or residence as well as belonging to a church whose character should shine as a beacon of light, showing the fruits of the Spirit.[2] Such a church shows what a community can be when it surrenders its will to the God of Love.

Rural churches have frequent opportunities to be agents of celebration and change when they help the whole local community to come together around a shared moment of triumph, disaster or endeavour. Such moments may relate to local individuals or to moving events such as the death of a princess, the village carnival, or a global crisis. The links that church people have with the daily life and concerns of their community can, with imagination, inspire an event that highlights the best aspects of life in community. In such moments or events the implicit faith that may be dormant in many can burst into life with a surprising freshness and hope.

Churches may be directly involved in the provision of publicly valued activities such as youth work or lunch clubs for the elderly. More frequently in rural areas, it is the case that church people make their contribution to community wellbeing through organizations that are not run by the church. Their personal networks and friendships are the vehicle by which they witness to the love of God, even if they do not openly state, or even know, that this is their motive. The 2006 report *Faith in Rural Communities* identified some of the range of contributions made to community life by the church:

> These contributions are, then, of various types: daily village living, networks with other churchgoers, formal worship opportunities, community activities organized through the church, activities organized through other village groups and the networks created through family, friendships, work and community service of one kind and another, including work with voluntary organizations and the parish council, for example.[3]

Christians take their responsibilities in society seriously, and are found in notable numbers holding office in a range of voluntary or statutory organizations.[4] One rural church invited congregation members to identify the nature of their involvement in community life. It transpired that 25 members were holding office in 31 local organizations. The realization of the potential of this influence for good gave fresh impetus to the church, the office holders, and to community organizations working for the economic and cultural regeneration of that area. Local churches benefit from building on this overlap of membership and involvement in community. The intercessions in worship can reflect the support of the congregation for what its members are doing during the week. The local church gains by having its vision of its own mission enlarged by hearing from those who serve the community in such a rich variety of ways. People who see their life beyond the church as the locus for their faith may welcome the support, understanding and prayers of their church. Many are informal carers and exemplars of good neighbourliness. They are the salt of the earth as Jesus described, and may need encouragement and support in what can be hard and time-consuming tasks.

Church people may be pulled in several directions for their available time. Their commitment to voluntary work in or for the church may conflict with their wider community involvement. In an ideal world, a balance would be struck that respected and supported their work in the community as well as in the church.

Not all churches behave alike. One church may have healthy interconnectedness that leads to co-operation in village events. This can reflect a positive relationship, a mutual support and relatedness that serves the kingdom of God in that community. Another church might maintain an unhealthy isolation and disconnection from the wider community. For example, no members of its PCC may serve on the village hall or sports club committees, and no one is involved in other community events. This leads to clashes of dates, debilitating competition and conflict. Here, the cause of the kingdom is not advanced as the link between faith and life is not expressed to the wider community, but is confined to the church, rather than being shared outside the household of faith.

In a discussion on the nature of community, the Archbishops' Commission on Rural Areas reported: 'For the Church to be truly committed to enabling persons to grow will involve the task of ensuring that society is organised in such a way that human beings can enter freely into these relationships of spiritual and material exchange that we call loving relationships.'[5]

Michael Langrish urges 'creative co-operation with agencies such as police, post office, health and social services, banks and so on'.[6] He argues that the church is a force for good in the wider rural society, and needs to have a prophetic voice. The church notice board, which should be at the boundary of the churchyard so that it can be read by passers-by, can be a powerful communicator of the church's message. It can display up-to-date information, including local contact people, notices about community events, as well as church information. Space inside the church can be used to show how partnership working is helping the quality of life for all in the community. Every effort is needed to show that the church exists for the good of all and that it is not a private club.

Such a church acts as the soul of a community. Both individuals and communities thrive when the soul receives regular care and attention:

Religious belief and faith has, by its nature, both personal and public dimensions. In relation to public benefit, it is the public dimension that is of primary importance. Where religion helps to provide a moral and ethical framework for people to live by, it can play an important part in building a better society.[7]

This recognition by the Charity Commission, an important public body, is welcome as society comes to value the positive contribution made by the church in rural areas to the fundamental well-being of the wider community, by its continuing presence as a praying, caring and worshipping community.

Size

Size is a two-edged sword. On the one hand, the intimacy of small groups can be a real benefit. On the other, it may lack sufficient strength to give confidence to try new things or attract new people. It is not just the churches that struggle to serve small groups or populations. Service providers in the public and private sectors also encounter difficulties in maintaining a rural presence.

Size of population is related to sparcity. Small populations will probably be spread out and further from centrally provided amenities, which will be in the larger villages and towns. Many rural communities have lost nearly all their familiar amenities. Hundreds of pubs, shops and garages have closed as their income has declined. The provision of health services, post offices and schools are subject to strict financial discipline that tends not to appreciate the impact of the withdrawal of services. Small rural communities may also be remote, exacerbating the impact on residents who have to be fit enough to be able to travel to reach vital services. Quite often the centralizing of a public service, such as a school or medical service, transfers some of the cost from the service provider to the customer. The increased travel involved in accessing the service is now borne by the parent or patient. This may also reduce the quality of the service provided. For example, the trend to centralization of hospital services reduces the access to consultants and increases 'Dead on Arrival' statistics from remoter rural areas.[8] Ambulances may take so long to reach emergency cases that they may not reach the Accident and Emergency Department in time.

Frustration is often voiced by church authorities that people are reluctant to travel to worship in other parishes. This hidden desire to centralize worship misses the point: that worship is, for many, an activity that is close to the heart and home, part of the place where they may have deep attachment. Where the congregation is drawn from all the parishes in the new grouping, more effort may be needed to retain the links between the church and its local community.

Smallness in relation to church congregations has no agreed definition, which may range from fewer than 25 members up to 200 members, in different denominations and countries. If 25 is taken as a benchmark, then there may be thousands of churches in rural settlements that will be thought of as small.

One assumption in diocesan strategic planning may be the wish to create a critical mass by linking together several small churches to form enough worshippers in one unit to support a paid priest. Such ecclesiastical joinery is often thwarted by the realities on the ground where people may not share the wish to form such a large unit. In the Church of England, churches that are overly dependent on the presence of or oversight by a priest have found survival hard in the face of the reduction in clergy numbers. Policy that sees clergy as the *sine qua non* of church life implements the logic of church closure until there are enough members to support the clergy. What is not assured is that closure of churches leads to transferred membership to stronger or larger churches. Anecdotal evidence from the Methodist experience suggests that church closure leads to reduced rather than transferred membership. Lewis Burton shows how this happened in the West Yorkshire Methodist District between 1970 and 2000 – the loss of members was larger than the closure of chapels would have suggested.[9] Research by Carol Roberts and Leslie Francis into church closure and membership statistics in four dioceses suggests that closure leads to declining attendance.[10] When small churches are linked into larger groups, identifying the special contribution that each can make to the whole may be one way of helping each church to gain pride and self-confidence.

The importance of volunteers is widely acknowledged. Most voluntary organizations, including the churches, need volunteers to take responsibility for a range of tasks. Many organizations, especially small churches, report difficulty in finding sufficient volunteers despite 27% of the population being actively engaged in regular formal volunteering.[11] There are certainly difficulties in recruiting volunteers to take on local leadership roles when there are only a handful of regular church attenders. Legally, a parish must find two churchwardens, a treasurer and secretary in addition to the other roles carried out by volunteers. One obstacle for churches may be the level of responsibility asked of office holders, particularly when there are few people available. The range of tasks needed, from cleaners to treasurer, requires several committed people. It is not healthy for an organization if one person carries out many roles. Music, work with children or young people, outreach and inspiration all suffer when leadership is left to a priest who visits on an occasional basis.

In nearly every settlement a church or chapel remains. To enable this to continue it may be necessary to bring together parish churches in a structure in which some churches are retained by being Chapels of Ease. This chapter uses the notion of 'cluster' to describe the variety of forms these structures can have (these are examined in more detail in the next section). One benefit that can come from linking churches together into larger clusters is that responsibility can be shared through a decision-making body that straddles several churches, enabling struggling churches to remain active without the requirement to provide a full set of office holders.

Michael Winter and Chris Short suggest that while many people who are listed on church membership rolls may use the terms 'Anglican' and 'Christian' as a way of indicating their identity, a low proportion show any active involvement by attendance at worship, with perhaps only 20% of those on the roll attending, apart from on special occasions.[12] A church with falling membership and reduced attendance may still be able to keep a place of worship open but, if it is infrequently used for worship or seldom used for activities by other groups, this can mask the reality that the Christian mission in that place may need to re-start in a new form.

Systems of communication between diocese and local churches and among those clustered churches require careful consideration. Ministering to small numbers is spiritually challenging for those whose model of church is of several hundred in the congregation, but the intimacy and mutual support that the handful can display can be a counterweight to the disappointment. 'For where two or three are gathered in my name, I am there among them'[13] are among Jesus' most important words on the nature of being church, and they have particular resonance for small congregations.

Full churches may be the experience of church policy makers from suburban churches, and of bishops when on their round of confirmations even if, in their head, they know the reality is otherwise. The normal experience of the rural parish priest is of small congregations in large buildings – far from the picture portrayed on television's religious programmes. However, that small congregation may be a far higher percentage of the population than is realized in what are thought of as successful suburban churches. Some rural congregations can, on special occasions, represent over three-quarters of the population, while a regular attendance of up to 10% is known – an undreamed-of possibility in larger parishes.

The positive benefit of working with very small numbers is countered by the recognition that for many people the idea of being in such a small congregation may not be attractive, particularly for young people. What is needed is activity appropriate to the number, the personalities and the context of that group of people. One very small settlement took the opportunity to encourage the handful of local young people to take a lead in design and delivery of worship, which is now valued by the whole benefice. Such bold measures can bring new life, hope and faith. Experience in the Scottish Episcopal Church shows how very small gatherings of worshippers can be helped, by an external consultant, to relate constructively to their local situation, offering worship that is sustainable and engaging in mission locally.[14]

Reflecting on scripture we can see how faith is not easily defeated by small numbers. The weak, the threatened and the small are encouraged to hold on and to endure, but also to be willing to make a new start, which may mean turning one's back on the past and the familiar. In the Old Testament, Gideon's experience of reducing his fighting force of volunteers to a smaller number of those who were really ready for the fight,[15] or Abraham's pleading to save Sodom by virtue of just ten righteous residents,[16] are examples of this. Jesus sees the potential of the smallness of the mustard seed,[17] the small offering of the boy's lunch,[18] and the significance of the widow's small gift.[19]

Small churches are usually linked with others to provide support, strength and the potential for enhanced activity – as we see in the next section.

Churches linking for ministry and mission

This section explores how the new larger clusters of parishes have been established, a development that has challenged congregations and clergy alike. Clergy are asked to work with churches that will have diverse characteristics and history. Parishes in rural areas have normally been linked together so that the priest, provided by the diocese, ministers to all who reside in those parishes. They have responsibility for worship within the churches of those parishes, but lay people are also called on to play a more significant role. Old linkages are replaced by new ones with larger numbers of churches involved.

There is a variety of structures in which groups of parishes are now clustered together. Many clusters of parishes are complex amalgams of previous pastoral arrangements and are groups of parishes and benefices held together, 'in plurality', as it is known. Alternatively, two or more benefices or parishes may be brought together into a new structure of a *united benefice*. These complex situations mean that every parish retains its own PCC and finances with the multiple meetings that this entails. In addition, a benefice council or joint churchwardens meeting may also take place. A *united parish* can bring together two or more parishes, replacing the separate PCCs for each parish with a single PCC for the cluster of parishes. The united parish can have one or more parish churches and one or more chapels of ease which remain open for public worship, but do not require churchwardens or a separate PCC. Each church may also have a district church council (DCC) to which certain powers or responsibilities can be delegated,[20] as is the case for a *team ministry*. A team ministry brings together several, usually a larger number of, parishes and clergy under the leadership of a team rector with one or more team vicars, who may take responsibility for sub-groups of churches within the team. A *group ministry* enables different clusters of parishes to work together so that clergy are licensed to work in all the parishes (as an assistant minister) and not just in their own parishes.[21] For the average parishioner, this complexity of structures may be bewildering as their loyalty is primarily, and sometimes solely, to their local parish church.

Churchwardens meeting from across the parishes can become a unifying group, both in planning and sharing the mission opportunities. To win allegiance from Christians in the parishes as well as from the diocesan authorities, the mission or service benefits of such flexibility will need to be clear. One of the tensions in these clusters is that of loyalty. Do church members belong to the local church or to the cluster? Does the newly coined name for the cluster help in presenting the church's mission to the wider world? However, the critical mass generated by such clustering may help most in tackling a social issue that would be beyond the capacity of a church on its own.

The logistics of distance, cost and time, and not just for the clergy, are issues that need considering when creating such large clusters. Each church may have something of unique value to offer. It may be helpful for one church in a cluster to specialize, for example, in youth work, Book of Common Prayer services, music, young children's work, or linking with the secondary school. Such a strategic approach can help small congregations to see that they have an important part to play in the bigger picture and help mitigate the feeling that choice has been surrendered in the new structure.

Whichever structure is created, it must be the result of wide and deep consultation so that the result is appropriate to the local context and local needs. Not enough is yet known about these various structures to be sure which works most effectively in support of the different aspects of the church's work in rural areas. The creation of some benefices may sometimes be a matter of what is possible rather than what is desirable.

The Dioceses, Pastoral and Mission Measure 2007 (DPMM)[22] is a very comprehensive piece of legislation which, among other provisions, offers parishes and benefices greater flexibility in adapting or changing existing structures and creating new ones; simplifies the process of closing a church building for regular public worship; and helps facilitate new local mission initiatives. The DPMM makes it easier to change local organizational arrangements – for example, by creating a united parish or a team ministry. It encourages flexible arrangements across parish and benefice boundaries and ecumenically, such as groups of parishes or benefices agreeing a covenant in order to work together more creatively. It also allows for the formation of group ministries across two or more benefices or teams, and encourages dual licensing of clergy – for example, across a deanery.[23]

Bishops' mission orders are a major part of the DPMM. They are intended to affirm, enable and support a new mission initiative or fresh expression of church within the wider life of the church, as well as to give it a legal status, offer oversight and encourage partnership working. This may be because the mission initiative is functioning across existing boundaries or that a new worshipping community has been formed, and where it would be appropriate for it 'to determine its own direction and life in collaboration within the parish in which it is set'.[24] A good example from the rural context would be: 'a network community that grows up within an existing multi-parish benefice, which, as part of its own growth to maturity, requires a similar legal status and recognition to that of the individual parishes within that benefice'.[25] The willingness to experiment with structures may be long overdue. Effective mission will rely not just on clergy and their supervisors, but on the commitment of those whose loyalty has been to traditional ways of working as well as those who want to be more adventurous for the gospel.

The contemporary struggle to provide sufficient clergy and supporting finance is not new. What is new is the surge of authorized lay leadership and vocations to non-stipendiary forms of ordained ministry, ensuring continuity of ministry in worship, work with children and young people, pastoral care and mission. The extent of this development is variable. Even if diocesan policy is to urge lay people to take leadership of worship and local mission work, some congregations may be hesitant to accept ministry and the leading of worship by lay people. Many have seen the benefit of extending ministry so that it belongs to all the baptized. In this latter view, the role of the clergy is to be inspirational, encouraging and to offer oversight of the laity as they exercise their ministry.

It is clear that training for clergy who are to lead the church's mission in such clusters has not yet been developed adequately. One central element that has to be learned is how to build teams of volunteers and how to support those who will be the leaders in their local church. This aspect of ministry is sometimes called *episcope*, oversight. The model of the relationship between bishop and clergy can thus be applied to that between priest and others engaged in ministry. It is one of trust, partnership in ministry, and a mutual development of skills. Both leaders and congregations adjust to a relationship in which ministry is shared, with the leader having a spiritual and practical oversight, and care for those who now share the ministry that once was theirs alone.

In recent decades there has been a dramatic reduction in the numbers of free church chapels in rural areas, with ministers tending to live in and operate from a nearby town. This emphasizes the fact that in many places the Anglican church may now be the only one present. Those who allocate resources in the Church of England would do well to recognize this fundamental difference with the urban situation. This puts obligations and responsibilities on the Church of England's rural clergy. Many Anglican congregations will include people who may still belong to another denomination. The recognition of and hospitality to ministers and members of other denominations is a positive step in sharing the gospel of Christ. Full recognition and partnership with other denominations at parish, deanery and diocesan level, working in rural areas, paves the way for a unified Christian mission. The breaking of old boundaries offers a fresh opportunity to think and act ecumenically. Learning to link with other churches can helpfully expand to include churches of other denominations. Local ecumenical partnerships[26] may not be possible everywhere, but even if no other church is present there will be Christians of other traditions living in the area and their contribution to the overall mission can be recognized. The Declaration of Ecumenical Welcome[27] does much to bring together in love and trust Christians of different traditions. Strategic thinking and planning at diocesan and regional level, as well as operational level agreements between individual churches, can pave the way for concerted Christian action and witness.

There is growing realization of the importance of good administration in the complexity of the multi-church situation. This is not generally a task for which clergy are prepared or equipped. Communication with the diocese is complicated when several churches are involved. There is a welcome and growing use of paid administrators at local level. This can be seen as more than help for the vicar, as it can fill a gap in organizational effectiveness. Full use can be made of new technology to ensure that all churches are included directly in the flow of information that is needed in a complex system of a cluster of churches.

Worship

This section identifies some of the issues involved in maintaining a good and diverse pattern of worship, but also the importance of both regular worship and special or seasonal services. Worship remains the core activity of the church and provides a focus for the whole community. The significance of the occasional offices in rural churches cannot be overestimated.

Over the past 50 years there has been a significant change in many rural churches in the way in which worship is arranged and delivered. Driven by the reduced availability of clergy, worship has both become less frequent in each church and at the same time increasingly led by lay people. However, Christian worship is still well placed to help rural people focus their spiritual journey.

Rural spirituality seems still to be readily in tune with the cycle of the natural year. Harvest and rogation special services attract significant numbers in addition to the regular attenders, particularly when the worship takes place in an appropriate setting such as a barn or even outdoors. Leslie Francis and I found that in communities of varying size, the average attendance at harvest was very similar to that of the carol service.[28] There is opportunity to link worship such as summer festivals or animal services with community events which make it easier for those on the fringe of congregational life to attend services and worship. Belief and uncertainty should not be taken to be in opposition, but seen more as part of a continuum. Rural churches often find success in providing worship occasions that help many to work through this continuum without embarrassment. They are also well placed to express faith as a shared experience rather than the contemporary emphasis on personal possession.

Occasional offices are of vital importance in rural communities. Here the church is on public show for one of its main purposes in the eyes of many residents. Funerals and weddings in rural areas may be less frequent than in more populous areas, but they are community events of great significance and can take up a large part of a priest's day. Appreciating the importance of the funeral for the whole community, and not just the family, can help give a priest a reputation as a good pastor. The warmth, tidiness and amenities the church building offers will be much appreciated. Local church policy and practice on baptism sets a tone for how the church is perceived and its mission accepted or resisted.

Good links into the community and an ability to use traditional forms as well as imagination in worship design are key elements of rural ministry. Clergy may find that on a typical Sunday they may use several different service forms ranging from the Book of Common Prayer to innovative family worship. The predominance of Holy Communion in previous decades is giving way to new forms that can appeal to new generations of worshippers.

The careful use of sound and light can enhance worship to great effect even when few are present. Many have come to deep spiritual experience in medieval churches when they are used to their full potential. While it is not possible to emulate a cathedral choral service, the worship must be appropriate to the setting and the numbers present. Paul Lack writes: 'All-age worship, using ordinary, day-to-day language and informal music, can express "immanence", while more "liturgical" services, with more formal language, can express "transcendence."'[29]

In times past a single rural church may have had more than one act of worship on a Sunday, allowing for different styles and emphases. Such choice, for traditional or non-eucharistic, or for modern worship may now only be possible across the cluster of churches.

The importance of predictable and consistent service times remains.[30] Local people may not readily be attracted to attend worship if the time of that service is not easily known. The way that churches inform local residents of the service pattern through the parish newsletter, local paper or website needs to be unambiguous, clear and simple.

One of the growth areas in church life is the increase in the number and range of people now leading worship. Most dioceses have active programmes of recruiting, training and authorizing lay people to lead worship, and the experience of worship led by lay people is steadily becoming more accepted by congregations. Research in 1988, 2000 and 2007 shows that clergy are generally supportive of lay-led worship. This mirrors the attitude of most lay members, although it is not always easy to find and train people for this task.[31]

There are several thousand readers on whom rural parishes have relied for many years. Alongside reader ministry, there are a growing number of non-stipendiary ministers who may still be in secular employment. Many benefices rely on help from retired clergy as well as non-stipendiary clergy to maintain their pattern of worship. Many dioceses offer house for duty posts as a way of providing support to full-time clergy, but with the ageing of the post-war baby boom generation of clergy, at least one diocese reports that the filling of all these posts is becoming difficult.

Worship is the core public activity of the church. Even when there are few participants, public worship can have a quality that brings people to their knees in awe and wonder of Almighty God.

Church buildings

This section addresses some of the key aspects of the witness enshrined in the building. The presence of the church building can be a powerful focus for mission within the community, but can also be a distraction from that mission. There is a growing awareness of the potential for multi-functional use of this important community asset, by the local community and by tourists and visitors.

Many rural settlements can be located from afar by virtue of the church tower or spire protruding above the surrounding landscape, and a large proportion of rural church buildings are listed or are historic structures – a powerful witness to the longevity of the Christian witness in rural areas. The ongoing demand of maintenance can distract attention from mission within the community, and those who love the church building may need reminding that over the centuries it has been subject to regular and sometimes dramatic adaptations in response to social, economic, political, as well as theological changes of emphasis. What is felt to be the traditional layout of sanctuary, chancel with choir and organ is in fact relatively recent. As re-orderings take place the empty space provided by the ancient structure can take on new forms that excite and stimulate the imagination. Even with no re-ordering, good use can be made of the old furniture. A farmers' market in one church is provided for by placing trestle tables for a few hours each week on the pew backs.[32]

A sea change is under way in hundreds of churches. Toilets, kitchens, modern heating and lighting are being provided within adapted and multi-functional churches to enable a wide range of community activities to take place. While the technology may be new, the purpose is not. It provides the church with an opportunity to engage anew with the local community. The energy and vision to make this sort of provision necessitates full community consultation. This will not be without conflict and disagreement. It will in turn, and in time, lead to greater understanding and support from the community of what the church is trying to be and to do.

Half the churches serving populations less than 3,000 are used for concerts;[33] others have made provision for playgroups, lunch clubs and IT training. In some, the nave has been handed over officially to serve as the village hall while the whole church continues as a place of worship.[34] There is growing and useful experience of making use of part of the church building as a post office or community shop.[35]

One diocese reports that 75% of the rural parish churches were open daily for prayer and quiet reflection.[36] The Christian faith is founded on belief in an incarnated God, who is found in the ordinary stuff of life as well as in the deep mysteries of thought and imagination. Local churches have opportunity to open the door into both the transcendent God and God who is made known in human form. It is the task of this generation to continue the tradition of presenting the place of worship as a place for such bi-fold encounter.

Many churches focus on offering a place of quiet and prayer. One well-visited church has reoriented the layout of the nave to make prayer easier by creating special and well-resourced spaces for prayer that are clearly signposted.[37] It is clear from comments in church visitors' books and responses to a sur-vey conducted for the then National Churches Tourism Group (now the Churches Tourism Association) that the desire to pray or spend time thinking is a valuable contribution to the well-being of many people, particularly locals.[38]

The encouragement from General Synod in July 2008[39] to dioceses to do more in relation to tourism builds on work that has been steadily growing to help churches respond to the sig-nificant number of people who want to visit churches. Not only are the churches of England one of the reasons given by over-seas visitors for coming to Britain, but they provide a place for reflection, and even sanity, in lives of those who may be troubled, as well as a window for all into the eternal realities.

It is welcome that so many more churches are being opened to help the millions of visitors who come through the doors become pilgrims.

Values

Four main values are identified that, although not in themselves peculiar to the rural church, nonetheless form a vital contribution to the church's witness. These values are the importance of relationships, significance of place, acceptance of diversity and service of others.

Relationships

At the heart of Christian belief is God as Trinity. Three Persons in One God. The significance of this seemingly complicated doctrine for the rural church becomes clear. As these different expressions of the One God relate together in harmony and unity, so does the rich variety of humanity discover its essential unity as part of God's creation. God as Creator is readily perceived in the natural world: the fields, trees, wildlife and landscape, hills, woods, rivers and seas. The natural environment that surrounds so many rural churches and fills their churchyards can provide a focus for worship and for people to find fresh contact with God. The way the church, as both people and the building, relate to the surrounding world shows the offer of salvation and the good news of redemption.

Place

The Creator God is also revealed to us in the human form of Jesus of Nazareth, born in a particular place at a particular time. This incarnation of divinity shows how what is created, including humanity, is also the arena for God's love and longing. Place can be about many things and encompasses both location and value. John Inge draws a difference between space and place. Space, he comments, is more abstract than place, and reflects our understanding of 'outer space' and of infinity. Place is more about 'locality, a particular spot'. 'What begins as undifferentiated space becomes place as we get to know it better and endow it with value. . . . What is undifferentiated space becomes for us significant place by virtue of our familiarity with it.'[40]

Familiarity with the particular location where we live leads to a sense of both identity and belonging for many people. The story the community tells about itself will be significant in defining that place. Knowing and understanding the importance of the story is as essential as knowing and understanding the people.

The rural church is located in and identified with the natural environment as well as with the local community. Many have been able to choose to live in rural areas, while others have been born into it. The church may have different perspectives for these two groups. It is, though, the place for all people to come to the fullness of God. Woodcarvers, designers, painters, glaziers, bellfounders and masons express this through their handiwork. Musicians, bellringers, flower-arrangers, cleaners and churchwardens carry on the worship of God in their daily care of the church.

Diversity

The Holy Spirit comes to us as a surprise, inviting us to try new things, new ways of celebrating the wonder and mystery of love. The three persons together show us the fullness of God. Constantly renewing, re-invigorating and leading into new ways of doing old things, the Spirit of God is at the heart of the church's mission. The diverse character and context of the churches that are linked together in rural areas mirror the diverse characteristics of the trinitarian God. Each can respect and enhance the others, bringing their distinctiveness and unique story together, thereby enriching the whole. To look for survival in independent autonomy is the way to a slow death.

Service of others

The example of the Christ from rural Galilee has inspired so much care for others, whether the one who does the caring is doing so explicitly as a committed Christian or because the culture of caring is an expression of humanity at its best. John Inge writes: 'If members of Christian communities could learn to be good neighbours to one another and to the larger communities of which they are a part, they would have something infinitely worthwhile to offer to the world. And it would be the very best form of evangelization.'[41]

One way church people are known in their community is by the quality of their relationships, and the way a congregation expresses love, both among the members but also with those who are not members, is an outworking of the gospel. A good example is the way those who are different, in age, ability, colour, sexual orientation or politics, are included. This is more than mere acceptance. It is a mirror of the experience people of faith have of the way they are loved by God with a full expression of forgiveness. These values of love, forgiveness, acceptance and commitment to place are expressed in service of others, both near and far away, shining as lights in a world that can, at times, even in beautiful countryside, be very dark.

Conclusion

The rural church has, for over a millennium, helped shape and give identity to thousands of villages and small towns in the countryside, by providing a focus for rites of passage and belonging for all residents.

Religious faith is undergoing hard contemporary challenges, but the movement of the tide of English history, reflected in the ancient stones and stories of rural churches, offers assurance that steadiness and continuity can be found. An alert church council will ensure that its church is open, thereby providing a focus for people's search for meaning and purpose, whether they are regular worshippers or not. Even with small congregations and numerous churches linked together for oversight by clergy, valuable witness is born from the rich soil of the spirituality and quality of life of the faithful few. Some will find the God who is worshipped in awe and wonder; others will find the rural prophet from Galilee, seeing God's likeness in that face; yet others will be exhilarated by the movement of the Spirit and want to try new things and dance for joy. The rural church has room for them all.

Questions

1 How can the connections between church members and the life of the community be recognized, affirmed and supported?

2 What special worship services might be developed to celebrate the contribution of community organizations to local well-being?

3 How can the unique qualities and story of each of the churches in your cluster be shared and acknowledged?

Notes

1 Flora Thompson, *Lark Rise to Candleford*, Middlesex: Penguin Modern Classics, 1945, p. 209.

2 Galatians 5.22–26.

3 R. Farnell, J. Hopkinson, D. Jarvis, J. Martineau and J. Ricketts Hein, *Faith in Rural Communities: Contributions of Social Capital to Community Vibrancy*, Stoneleigh Park: Acora Publishing, 2006, p. 47.

4 Leslie Francis and Jeremy Martineau, *Rural Mission*, Stoneleigh Park: Acora Publishing, 2002, p. 115.

5 Archbishops' Commission on Rural Areas, *Faith in the Countryside*, Worthing: Churchman Publishing, 1990, p. 23.

6 Michael L. Langrish, 'Dynamics of community', in Jeremy Martineau, Leslie J. Francis and Peter Francis (eds), *Changing Rural Life: A Christian Response to Key Rural Issues*, Norwich: Canterbury Press, 2004, p. 34.

7 Charity Commission, *The Advancement of Religion for the Public Benefit*, London: Charity Commission, 2008, p. 3, http://www.charity-commission.gov.uk/Library/publicbenefit/pdfs/pbreligiontext.pdf (accessed 1 April 2009).

8 Iain J. Mungall, *Ensuring Equitable Access to Health and Social Care for Rural and Remote Communities. Increasing Centralisation and Specialisation within the NHS: The Trend Has Some Adverse Effects on Access to Care for Rural and Remote Communities*, 2006, pp. 4–5, http://www.rural-health.ac.uk/publications/mungall-equitable-access.pdf (accessed 27 March 2009).

9 Lewis Burton, 'Church closure and membership statistics: a Methodist perspective', *Rural Theology*, 5(2), Issue 69, 2007, pp. 125–36.

10 Carol Roberts and Leslie J. Francis, 'Church closure and membership statistics: trends in four rural dioceses', *Rural Theology*, 4(1), Issue 66, 2006, pp. 37–56.

11 Volunteering England Information Sheet, *National Statistics*, London: Volunteering England, 2008, p. 3, http://www.volunteering.org.uk/NR/rdonlyres/1F9DB0E1-A0DB-421E-B3C3-674BFD9772BF/0/NationalStatisticsVE083.pdf (accessed 1 April 2009).

12 Michael Winter and Chris Short, 'Believing and belonging: religion in rural England', *British Journal of Sociology*, 44, 1993, pp. 635–51.

13 Matthew 18.20.

14 Scottish Episcopal Church, *Local Collaborative Ministry: The Story So Far*, Edinburgh: Scottish Episcopal Church, 2008.

15 Judges 7.

16 Genesis 18.23–32.

17 Mark 4.31–32.

18 John 6.5–13.

19 Luke 21.2–4.

20 *Church Representation Rules*, London: Church House Publishing, 2006.

21 See the Pastoral Measure 1983, as amended by subsequent legislation including the Dioceses, Pastoral and Mission Measure 2007, pp. 24–31, http://www.cofe.anglican.org/about/churchcommissioners/pastoralandclosedchurches/commonresources/pastoralmeasure/pastoral measure1983.doc (accessed 1 April 2009).

22 Dioceses, Pastoral and Mission Measure 2007, http://www.cofe.anglican.org/about/churchcommissioners/pastoralandclosedchurches/commonresources/dpmm/ (accessed 1 April 2009).

23 For comments and explanations of the Dioceses, Pastoral and Mission Measure 2007, see http://www.cofe.anglican.org/about/church-commissioners/pastoralandclosedchurches/commonresources/dpmm/dpmmnotes.doc (accessed 1 April 2009).

24 Dioceses, Pastoral and Mission Measure 2007 Part V: Mission Initiatives, Code of Practice, House of Bishops, 2008, pp. 1–2, http://www.cofe.anglican.org/about/churchcommissioners/pastoralandclosedchurches/commonresources/dpmm/dpmmcop.doc (accessed 1 April 2009).

25 Dioceses, Pastoral and Mission Measure 2007 Part V, p. 2.

26 For more information on local ecumenical partnerships, see http://www.cofe.anglican.org/info/ccu/england/leps/ (accessed 1 April 2009).

27 Council for Christian Unity, 'What if the Anglican Church Is the Only Church in my Village?', http://www.cofe.anglican.org/info/ccu/england/resources (accessed 1 April 2009).

28 Francis and Martineau, *Rural Mission*, p. 59.

29 Paul Lack, *All Mud and Matins? Understanding Rural Worship*, Grove Booklet W196, Cambridge: Grove Books, 2008, p. 11.

30 Archbishops' Commission on Rural Areas, *Faith in the Countryside*, pp. 188–9.

31 See: Douglas Davies, Charles Watkins and Michael Winter, *Church and Religion in Rural England*, Edinburgh: T & T Clark, 1991, pp. 156ff.; Leslie J. Francis, Keith Littler and Jeremy Martineau, *Rural Ministry*, Stoneleigh Park: Acora Publishing, 2000; Rural Ministry Survey by the Arthur Rank Centre for the Centre for Studies in Rural Ministry (unpublished).

32 Monica Long, 'Farmers market on the agenda', *Country Way*, Issue 37, 2004, Stoneleigh Park: Arthur Rank Centre, p. 7.

33 Unpublished research by the National Rural Officer for the Church of England in 1998.

34 Archbishops Council, The Pastoral (Amendment) Measure 2006, 'Wider use of part or parts of a Church', 2007, http://www.cofe.anglican.org/about/churchlawlegis/measures/pamguide.rtf (accessed 1 April 2009).

35 Guidelines and Best Practice for the Provision of a Hosted Post Office® Service in Churches and Chapels, 2008, http://www.churchcare.co.uk/develop.php?FF (accessed 1 April 2009).

36 Church Heritage Forum, *Building Faith in Our Future*, London: Church House Publishing, 2004, p. 29.

37 Great Budworth, Cheshire.

38 Leslie J. Francis and Jeremy Martineau, *Rural Visitors*, Stoneleigh Park: Acora Publishing, 2001, p. 84.

39 See GS misc 887A, Private Members Motion on Church Tourism, http://www.cofe.anglican.org/news/gsjul080706.html (accessed 1 April 2009).

40 John Inge, *A Christian Theology of Place*, Aldershot: Ashgate, 2003, pp. 1–2.

41 Inge, *A Christian Theology of Place*, p. 136.

3

Leadership models and skills

AMIEL OSMASTON

A clergy friend of mine who is in her late fifties was recently advised by a well-meaning acquaintance, 'Why don't you apply for one of those quiet little rural parishes, where it's not too demanding and you can start practising for retirement?' With difficulty, my friend restrained herself from biting the person's head off. I'm not sure that I could have been so restrained. My experience over the past 20 years with leadership training programmes for clergy and laity has given me the privilege of engaging with leaders in rural contexts whose ministries are incredibly varied, exciting and demanding.

Rural leadership is not an easy semi-retirement option. It calls for the ability to grow other people into leadership and to work closely with them. The range of leadership models that one is required to inhabit are usually more complex and multi-layered than in urban or suburban contexts. A rural leader, whether ordained or lay, has to move with swift sensitivity from being, for example, an entrepreneur at one moment to being more like a midwife or a farmer, a carpenter, a weaver, a storyteller or a parent at the next. These are the models of leadership that will be explored later in this chapter, which is written primarily for authorized church leaders: stipendiary and non-stipendiary clergy, ordained local ministers, readers, accredited lay ministers, churchwardens and other recognized lay leaders. Most of it is applicable to any denomination, and also more widely to rural leaders operating beyond the church.

It aims to:

- identify what is distinctive about leadership in rural contexts;
- explore seven imaginative models which are particularly characteristic of leadership in these contexts;
- identify some skills and personal qualities which are especially useful for rural leaders.

And also to offer:

- a deeper understanding of models of leadership which you may already be using unconsciously;
- encouragement to explore using new models;
- greater confidence about the relevance of the skills and qualities you already have, and ideas about additional skills that might be worth developing.

What sort of leadership?

Vast amounts have been written about leadership in general and about church leadership in particular. Broadly, the consensus is that it involves enabling a body of people to live, grow and journey together in a way that serves God's mission in that particular place. Within that broad definition, what sort of leadership is appropriate for rural multi-parish benefices?

Being a leader in a rural context is not slow, sleepy and old-fashioned. The countryside is changing fast and is at the cutting edge of many of the most challenging environmental issues currently facing humanity.

What is distinctive about rural leadership?

Rural leadership is corporate. Most rural parishes are now part of team or group ministries or large multi-parish benefices. For leaders, this involves complex multi-level decision-making processes. For clergy, it will probably also involve overseeing several communities and buildings. Clergy cannot be everywhere at once, so it becomes more obvious that other people need to be enabled to share in ministry and leadership.

Rural leadership is relational. The leader is relating to a network of people, not managing a system. Congregations are mostly fairly small so people tend to know each other and individuals are noticed. It is vital that the leader is seen to care about individuals in the church and wider community and is approachable, trustworthy and dependable. The leader's character and integrity will be carefully scrutinized.

How leadership is shaped by rural culture, attitudes and theology

Time

In rural cultures, time may be seen as cyclical (or spiral), based on the cycle of the seasons rather than just linear. This can cause problems for leaders who try to use methods of vision-forming that are based on traditional linear business models of strategic change. Country people may approach something new in an indirect and spiral manner. Furthermore, the commitments and obligations to the past are closely bound up with people's identity, so it is vital to understand the history of the area.

Place

Rural spirituality was forged by those who were in touch with the soil and the seasons.[1] Real locals with ancestors who have been rooted in the place for generations are increasingly rare, but still influential. Nowadays, though, incomers who have bought into the area may be even more committed to celebrating and preserving it than villagers of long standing. At its worst, the threat to the innovating leader becomes: 'We paid a lot for this rural charm. Don't you dare change it.' Yet the rural vicar, in spite of usually being an outsider, represents the place and is called to serve and pray for it. The leadership has to be incarnational. 'The parish is quintessentially a "place". Its demise is increasingly predicted by a generation encouraged by our all-pervasive urban culture, desiring to live in the freedom given by "spaces".[2] In Walter Brueggemann's work *The Land*,[3] the author stresses that the land in which the Lord has set us should continue to be fundamental for God's people.

Priests

It is only fairly recently that leadership qualities have become a selection criterion for Anglican ordinands. However, laity in rural areas still tend to see clergy as priests responsible for the cure of souls, rather than as leaders. Also, some clergy feel called to a traditional pastoral ministry of holy presence and are uncomfortable about seeing themselves as leaders. The danger is that this avoidance of leadership can lead to a static, reactive, maintenance ministry.

Laity

Lay people often think of themselves as the vicar's helpers. Particularly in rural areas, there is a tremendous need to challenge this attitude and to affirm and build confidence, and a sense of lay vocation to mutual ministry and shared leadership. This leadership should not just be confined to activities within the church. In many rural areas there will be church members who commute to jobs that involve significant leadership responsibilities and national-level decision-making. The church can play a significant role in resourcing them to think and lead as Christians within their areas of responsibility.

God

In rural congregations there is usually a strong emphasis on seeing God as creator, preserver and sustainer, and clergy are expected to preach this and to reflect these qualities in their leadership. This is fine as far as it goes, but misses the themes of salvation and redemption so critical to the gospel. Furthermore, as Bishop David Jenkins wrote:

Is it the calling of faithful Christian communities and churches to protect and preserve unchanged understandings of God's revelation *in the past*, or to perceive and promote God's promises and calling for the *future*? . . . God has *not* stopped. He is the living God and he goes on with his revelation, his encounters, his calling, his creativity and his promises.[4]

Leaders need to be aware of the characteristics of God they reflect in exercising their leadership. There is a danger of over-emphasizing some characteristics and neglecting others in order to collude with the congregation's comfort zone. For example, rural churches tend to be traditional in outlook, so members may be uncomfortable with aspects of theology that they perceive as disturbing or divisive – such as the work of the Holy Spirit or God as Judge.

Mission

In rural areas faith is often implicit, shown in practical works and relationships within the community. In a stable community people are often unwilling to do anything that differentiates them from everyone else. Church members may not want to be distinctive or to stand out, since this is seen as divisive. People who have been brought up locally may find it difficult to challenge the personal faith of relatives and lifelong neighbours. This means that the forms of mission need to be largely communal, rather than associational or individualistic, aiming to draw the whole community into faith and discipleship. Being a rural leader in mission can be rather like evangelizing a tribe without knowing who the chief is.[5]

The call to lead together

The gifts he gave were that some would be apostles, some prophets, some evangelists, some pastors and teachers, to equip the saints for the work of ministry, for building up the body of Christ until all of us come to the unity of the faith and of the knowledge of the Son of God, to maturity, to the measure of the full stature of Christ (Ephesians 4.11–13).

To achieve this high calling, everything that we do as church must be corporate, including our leadership. Church growth requires shared ministry and leadership, and rural leadership cannot be a solo performance. It must be a collaborative process of leading together.

Rural congregations have some very long-standing members, unlike urban congregations where there may be more mobility. Some families in rural areas may have attended the church for generations. The congregation will usually outlive individual clergy, even if they are in post for a couple of decades. This means that in the countryside it is even more important for the whole congregation to be seen as the local agents of mission and ministry, and it is vital that clergy do not zoom in like Superman and take over this role. The responsibility of the leader is to build up long-term local collaborative leadership.

This will require skills to discern gifts in other people. It will also require affirming, encouraging, building confidence, training, resourcing, supervising, collaborating, giving responsibility and empowering people to take on appropriate ministries and leadership roles. This may indicate that the practice of oversight ministry, episcope, is paramount. People usually find it difficult to discern their gifts. A six-session course for small groups, to help discover gifts and abilities, 'Your Shape for God's Service',[6] has been effectively used for this purpose in many parishes throughout Britain.

Rural clergy in multi-parish contexts can be in the position of overseeing a team of other leaders, both clergy and lay, training, enabling and supporting them. This means resisting the temptation to control or do everything oneself, and instead to give away power and responsibility to others. Collaboration is more than mere delegation. It involves partnership, acknowledging and working with differences, mutual feedback and open communication. Given the breadth of churchmanship in most rural congregations, the leadership or ministry team may contain members with very different church traditions. It can be challenging to forge a sense of mutual trust and unity, but the diversity will enable a much richer range of ministry than in a more monochrome church. In a multi-parish situation some churches will probably move ahead faster than others, so that preserving unity can feel like straddling several horses in a Roman chariot race. It is important not to allow one church to block the progress of the others.

Providing eucharistic worship in a multi-parish benefice has usually required clergy to have the flexibility and stamina to take multiple services, reflecting different traditions in a variety of different venues. One vicar commented that this required a thermal vest, a good bladder, a reliable car, a family that don't expect Sunday lunch, and at least one committed church-warden on every site to set up and clear away afterwards. This rushing around is obviously not ideal and allows no time for relationship-building before and after services. Therefore in a multi-parish context it is particularly important for readers and teams of lay leaders to be trained to lead various appropriate forms of worship or take responsibility for welcome, hospitality and pastoral care.

Clergy are often given greater community status and influence in rural areas than in urban or suburban contexts. However, it is important not to misuse this. The need to dominate or control, or to be a large fish in a small pond, can be fatal for effective leadership. Rural people tend to prize humility above self-confident assertiveness. The less direct or overt faces of power will be more effective, such as networking, influencing, persuading and negotiating. Daniel Goleman, who has written extensively on the subject of emotional intelligence, argues that leadership is not domination, but the art of persuading people to work towards a common goal.[7] In this book, Goleman sees the quality of empathy, developed through self-control, social awareness and social skill, as particularly vital for persuading and motivating people.

Growing collaborative leadership

Many Anglican dioceses have set up programmes to encourage parishes to develop new forms of collaborative ministry and leadership. These go by various names, such as mutual ministry, total ministry, leadership teams, local ministry development groups. There is a significant international movement and an extensive literature on the subject.[8]

Growing patterns of collaborative leadership requires persistence and hard work. It can be blocked by clergy who are unable to let go of power and control, but it can also be blocked by congregations that do not want to take on the responsibilities of leadership. Groups that are anxious tend to look for a superhero or all-powerful leader to save them from their anxieties. However, the hero always turns out to have feet of clay in the end and the anxieties return with renewed force.[9]

Many rural congregations are small and feel anxious about their own survival. Therefore they may be particularly vulnerable to seeking to appoint omni-competent clergy:

> The conferment of the leadership function on the heroic leader can lead to dependency and possibly indolence in the rest . . . When leadership of a system is a product of dependency, the system as a whole is diminished. The capacity of the community to shape its future, to organize its endeavour and to change itself in the doing, is reduced. If, however, leadership can be viewed as the goal of the system as a whole and the work of all in it, we begin to nurture, develop, build and sustain leadership capacity in the system as a whole.[10]

Building leadership capacity will involve drawing the whole congregation into a continuous process of reviewing and growing in shared vision (seeing together), putting vision into practice (walking together), and engaging in constructive dialogue (talking together).[11]

Leaders who wish to work in a more collaborative way need to devote considerable time to building relationships with their

gues, nurturing, resourcing and overseeing them. Ian
ims has done some interesting research on the kinds of
clergy–lay relationships that have enabled the development of
collaborative ministry and leadership.[12] These include:

- encouraging and supporting the personal development of
  others;
- clergy being open and being themselves, rather than always
  staying in role;[13]
- treating others as equals and partners in ministry;
- being open to new ideas and willing to innovate;
- seeking and inviting lay participation and involvement;
- leading in a way that gives a sense of direction and stability,
  but without being over-directive or prescriptive, and avoiding being *laissez-faire;*
- being encouraging and enthusiastic.

Jim Mynors says:

> St Paul's strategy was unashamedly focused on training key
> leaders for the future[14] . . . His multi-church ministry resulted
> in dramatic and lasting growth. The churches in Ephesus and
> Philippi were still around in the sixth century when the two
> cities were deserted. Corinth still has a church 2000 years
> on, and I believe there's one in Rome (!). Paul's strategy
> was about growth after he left, not just about survival. Why
> should we expect less today?[15]

Leaders or priests?

It should, of course, be 'and' not 'or'. All ordained priests who
have responsibility for one or more congregations need to be
able to be leaders. All Christian lay ministry and leadership
also has a priestly element to it. A priest is called to enable
the whole congregation to understand what it means for them
together to be God's 'holy priesthood' for their area, and how
to exercise a spiritual ministry as well as a practical one.[16]

An authorized church leader becomes a representative sacred person within the community, reflecting to the congregation the calling to holiness. It can be dangerous if the leader becomes instead a substitute sacred person (a particular danger for clergy). If this happens, the leader can disempower other people who may expect everything sacred and spiritual to be done by the leader. The congregation then see themselves as just there to help the leaders in practical ways. In the countryside, people are often wonderfully willing to offer practical help, but this helping mentality can be accompanied by low self-confidence and a fear of taking spiritual initiative or responsibility.

A leader is called to be holy, an example of grace and faith whose life of prayer and depth of relationship with God is fundamental. In the rural fishbowl, a leader who is disillusioned or cynical, in whom the spark of vocation has died, will be detected not just by the congregation, but by the wider community as well. In particular, clergy and their families are under close observation. A vicar new to rural ministry observed ruefully:

> In my last parish I could become anonymous and invisible simply by removing my dog collar, but that doesn't work here! I can't hide! People discuss and observe everything I do. Also, I can't separate my public and private selves. I have to let people get to know 'the real me' more openly here.

Clergy or lay leaders with a pastoral role are also entrusted with complex confidential information, and this is both a privilege and a burden. In the countryside, discretion and strict confidentiality are particularly important, as so many people are interrelated or likely to know each other. Any breach of confidentiality can very quickly destroy trust and so bring leadership into question.

Models and skills for rural leadership

I offer seven models of leadership that are particularly relevant to ministering in a rural context. These are complementary, not mutually exclusive, and all need to be exercised in order for the church to grow. However, they do not all need to be exercised by the clergy or by any single leader, and some work better in certain contexts or situations. Nobody is likely to feel equally at home in all of the models. Where there is shared leadership, it is useful to discern which leaders naturally use which skills and models – then each can concentrate on their particular strengths. When helping others to grow in leadership, an exploration of the different models may be useful in seeking to develop the relevant skills.

In relation to each model of leadership, certain skills and qualities are identified that are necessary for the leader to demonstrate in order to exercise a particular model. However, a few skills and qualities are so fundamental that they are necessary for every model of rural leadership. These are:

- An interest in and knowledge of the work, life and values of the countryside, which can often feel neglected, misunderstood and judged by government and society.
- An ability to use a range of leadership and ministry styles, as one is likely to be leading several very different churches.

Farmer

Farmers have the care of the livestock and the land and responsibility to sow the seed. They must know their land and its setting in order to enable the cycle of the year to be most fruitful – for example, in sowing and harvesting. Similarly, authorized church leaders have the cure of souls in that place and the responsibility to communicate the seed of the word of God. They must know their context, the gifts and resources available, and the right timing for action in order to enable the church or team to flourish.

At times, rural leadership may feel like ploughing concrete. It requires patience and taking the long-term view. One vicar commented: 'As a Cumbrian, I find that the Cumbrian people are not opposed to change, but they are totally opposed to being told to change'. So the wise leader will prepare the ground, choose the best season, drop seeds in the right places, and not over-water the seedlings. The needs and culture of the community must not be overridden, so the desire for change will probably have to grow slowly from the grassroots up. This stands in contrast to the viewpoint of John Kotter, who writes that for change to happen, it is essential to establish a sense of urgency.[17]

The farmer has to gain the trust of the flock by spending time with them and understanding them. Similarly, a leader must be alongside people as a patient listener. The farmer is also responsible for building up the health of the herd, developing its genetic qualities and strengthening its immunity from disease. Likewise, the leader has to nurture, teach and strengthen the congregation, so that its members develop a theological 'immune system'. Edwin Friedman says that just as the physical immune system detects and resists alien invaders and destructive viruses, so a congregation's immune system consists of the ability of the body to recognize and reject ideas or activities that are incompatible with their faith.[18]

Most farmers do not work entirely alone, and nor do Christian leaders:

> What then is Apollos? What is Paul? Servants through whom you came to believe, as the Lord assigned to each. I planted, Apollos watered, but God gave the growth ... For we are God's servants, working together; you are God's field (1 Corinthians 3.5–7, 9).

It is important for leaders to discern whether their particular strength is in the spiritual equivalent of:

- ploughing: challenging and changing the church's status quo;

- sowing: spreading new ideas;
- planting: starting new things;
- watering: enabling growth;
- weeding: removing blockages;
- or reaping: gaining final results.

Also, it is important to ask which of these is most needed at present in this church and community. Which role or phase is the leader called to? And how do their gifts and calling complement those of other leaders in the team?

Entrepreneur

The countryside has always been a place of adaptation, experimentation and entrepreneurial activity. Farmers and rural small businesses have to build on their existing assets, to diversify and respond rapidly to changes in the market and the economy. The rural church leader has to be entrepreneurial too. This will involve courageous risk-taking and stepping out in faith with contagious optimism and hope. Leaders who are new to rural life must not believe the false myth that country dwellers are stuck in the mud, conservative and unchanging.

However, the entrepreneurial leader's methods of managing change have to be different in a rural context. Compared with an urban setting, rural populations are smaller and people are more closely interconnected. Therefore good personal relationships and trust in the leader are absolutely crucial for enabling change. Time spent with individuals is vital, listening to their concerns about proposed changes, and getting them on board. People who are alienated by the change process cannot simply move to worship elsewhere when the nearest church outside their own benefice may be 35 miles away! Also, their anger will spread quickly within rural networks and cause resentment in the wider community towards the church.

However, the good news for rural leaders is that once the community believes that you know them, love them and want the best for them, they will work with you most effectively.

Most rural parishes have had to cope with more structural and leadership changes over the past few decades than urban parishes, with the formation of teams and groups and the loss of resident clergy. So the entrepreneur leader should expect that there may be a sense of insecurity and change-fatigue. However, once people do own an initiative, there is a great sense of loyalty and commitment in the countryside to making communal activities work.

To be entrepreneurial, leaders have to be patient and resilient, with a deep trust and faith in Christ. Like other rural entrepreneurs, they need to be able to pick themselves up and try again, to see new possibilities and identify new resources.

Storyteller

All communities have their storytellers who remember, re-tell and interpret the key events that give that community its particular history, character and identity. This role is mainly informal – exercised in the pub and in the Women's Institute. More formal local histories have often been written by parish clergy. This is not surprising, as one of the first tasks for a Christian leader moving into a new place is to discern how local people see their community, and the kind of stories they tell about themselves.

In a rural area, these stories may be more consistent and deep-rooted than in a mobile urban environment. The stories may need to be interpreted, affirmed or challenged. The church leader becomes a storyteller for individuals, the church and the wider community, building a culture and ethos, a sense of identity, meaning, purpose and vision. This involves inspiring people and helping them to see their lives within the overarching context of God's story of creation and redemption enacted in this place:

People are looking for meaning, and they respond much better to encouragement and example than to dictates. Effective leaders no longer command they tell stories – and I don't mean lies – but they show one group of people how another has faced, tackled and overcome particular issues . . . The leader doesn't do it – the people do it but by being shown the possibilities and doing it themselves.[19]

Like Jesus' parables, the stories can be effective agents of change. They may have an uncomfortable, challenging or even prophetic edge to them. The hearers may experience a shock of recognition, as they see themselves and their lives in a fresh light. If the truth of the story is rejected, the storyteller may also be rejected and crucified.

The future vision has to be drawn out of past history, so that the community can maintain its identity. In the countryside, the people who shaped the history, or their descendants, are probably still around. The storyteller will help people to engage with the implications of the story for this community, church and local key families. The leader may first have to identify and disentangle deep historical knots and hurts in the community, and this might involve sensitive pastoral care, appropriate confrontation, enabling representative confession, repentance and the forgiveness of wrongdoers.[20]

One country priest commented:

If I were to give one piece of advice to any new clergy person in a rural parish it would be: learn the story of the parish before you attempt major change. The way things are done may seem strange to you, but there is always a reason for it, perhaps hidden in the past. Get to know and understand the people and their community history. If people know you understand why they are the way they are, they are more likely to trust you when you ask them to consider a change.

To be an effective storyteller, the leader will need skills of listening and discernment, communication (harder within complex but scattered rural networks) and the ability to inspire and motivate people.

Another rural leader wrote to me:

We are shortly to have a Deanery Mission led by the Bishop. As part of the planning, we were determined to enable the people in the more isolated fellside parishes to own the mission and to respond in their way. We encouraged them to think about how Christianity was first brought to them and how it has been kept alive within their communities over the centuries. The process has certainly made us all more aware of the commitment and faithfulness of those early missionaries and all who have passed on the tradition.

Carpenter

A carpenter uses a lump of wood to create something useful, beautiful and lasting. The process of carving or turning a piece of wood brings out its unique beauty, enhancing the grain, working around the twists and knots in the wood, incorporating them into the finished design. In many ways, a rural leader is like the carpenter, in that it is vital to appreciate and work with the grain of the culture, not against it. The leader has to use the givens of the situation and the community, and build on them. In the same way, the carpenter leader identifies the positive aspects of rural culture, then strengthens and develops them.

A vicar wrote: 'Affirm the faith you find, and enhance it. It is important to be enthusiastic about the strengths you find, rather than critical and negative about the weaknesses.' So such a leader will shape, sandpaper and polish the strengths, but will not ignore the weaknesses, collude with people's refusal to change, or give in to opposition. A carpenter has to be firm but flexible. It is no good setting out to build a table and ending up with a chair. However, the characteristics of the wood will shape the kind of table that is eventually created. Similarly, it is no good setting out to build a church and ending up with a club. However, the local culture and community will shape the kind of church that is eventually created.

A creative leader can help the community to find new and spiritually engaging ways of working with the grain to celebrate aspects of their history and culture:

Instead of marking the Millennium on 1 January, we decided
to celebrate it a month later, on Candlemas. Traditionally
Candlemas was the quarter day when the farming tenancies
changed. The outgoing tenants left a fire burning in the grate
ready for the new tenants to move in during the afternoon.
At Candlemas, the community was used to moving from the
old things to the new. We designed a liturgy including a pro-
cession of lighted lanterns, music from a Celtic harpist, peni-
tence leading to a recommitment of faith and being sent out
as lights in the world. All we did was to articulate in a Christian way what was already happening in the community.

Parent

Being a good parent involves love and self-sacrifice, giving
time and commitment to building close relationships, training,
nurturing and growing the children. Similarly, being a leader
in a small and closely linked rural community is like a parent
socializing a family, in contrast to leading a large congregation,
which requires a more systemic and managerial approach. The
rural leader must commit themselves to gathering and nurturing people, to knowing and loving them, to helping them grow
in Christian understanding and life.

Rural ministry requires a major investment of oneself in relationships, which can be a strain for those who are naturally
introverts, as most clergy are. Like parents, leaders need to
be prepared to put down roots and give a considerable chunk
of time in order to build relationships and trust. Warmth and
consistency are vital to this enterprise. It is impossible to lead
people unless they trust you enough to go with you.

Rural leadership has sometimes been guilty of a patriarchal
approach, which can generate dependency. However, rather
than throwing the baby out with the bathwater, the model of
parent needs to be rehabilitated. Much interesting research has
been done on ways in which the principles of family therapy can
be applied to the emotional dynamics of congregations.[21] As in
a family, there may be sibling rivalry, triangulated relationships

and conflicts, grumbling, anxiety, and many other dysfunctional and immature forms of behaviour. The parent-leader needs wisdom to discern these behaviours, and the interpersonal skills for building and sustaining a mature, relational family system.

A great deal can be built on the pastoral emphasis of rural ministry, as long as one does not collude with the old expectation that the Vicar will do it all. Now that most rural clergy have several communities to care for, it is vital to identify and train lay people who have pastoral gifts and to build a recognized pastoral care team.

The leader's job is not primarily to do the work of ministry, but to equip the whole people of God for the work of ministry. Parent leadership is kenotic,[22] self-emptying, self-sacrificial, denying oneself, and putting others forward. As parents seek to help their children discover their gifts and grow into mature and independent adults, so the parent leader will seek to grow other leaders. Unfortunately, in some areas if a person puts themselves forward, others will say: 'Who does she think she is?' A good parent leader can create a positive and relaxed culture of having a go. It is important to accept the 'good enough' stance, and not strive to be a perfectionist. A sense of humour, and not taking oneself too seriously, also helps.

Weaver

In the weaver's hands, weak threads are brought together to form a firm, strong fabric. Seemingly random different-coloured strands are carefully incorporated, creating a clear and connected pattern. Similarly, in the countryside a church leader is a networker, creating connections, ensuring a close weave in the fabric of the community. The rural church leader is a leader of the whole community, not just of the local congregation. The role involves being a peacemaker, a bridgebuilder, a community reconciler, creating unity, collaboration and partnership. Rural leadership therefore tends to be inclusive rather than exclusive in style, cautious about taking sides or adopting strong positions.

Just as the weaver forms a multi-coloured pattern, a team leader draws different people in and helps them to find their place. There may be opportunities for creating and affirming ecumenical links. However, Anglican leaders will need to be ecumenically sensitive since there may be no churches of other denominations in more remote rural areas. A significant proportion of churchgoers in the countryside have previously been, or still are, members of other denominations. This can produce clashes between the different colourings of theology and approaches to leadership, but it creates a rich, diverse and exciting pattern of rural church life.

Midwife / layer-out

The local midwife, who was traditionally also the layer-out of corpses, was a vital member of the community and presided over life and death. Every person, high or low, would pass through her hands at the beginning and the end. Similarly, a church leader deals in beginnings and endings, providing the rites of passage for life and death. This is particularly true in rural areas, where the church usually has a large fringe with a higher than average attendance at baptisms, weddings and funerals. In the countryside many funerals still take place in the church and large numbers of the community will probably attend each one. It is more likely that the leader will already know the deceased and the bereaved family, which makes it more emotionally demanding.

Like the other models, that of the midwife / layer-out is not only for clergy. It is also particularly relevant for readers and for many lay leaders who are involved in preparation, visiting, training and follow-up for baptisms, weddings and funerals. These occasional offices are so important in the rural context because they are the way to build confidence and trust between church and community. This model expresses the being-alongside in birth and death that is so much part of parish work. A member of the clergy said to me: 'For one parishioner, I have taken the funeral service for her daughter, husband and mother, baptized her granddaughter and will shortly officiate at the marriage of her other granddaughter.'

A midwife helps a woman in labour, but in the end it is the mother who gives birth to the child. This also applies to leaders and congregations. The midwife leader does not take over and displace the ministry of others, but enables them to achieve something:

> After a year of meeting together for fellowship, prayer and fun, a group of ladies decided to start a small service for pre-school children and their carers. They plan and lead it as a team. Now young families come and make friends there; it is providing a route into church for some. The midwife for this group is a lay leader who simply asks questions such as 'What should we be doing?' and supplies the confidence and encouragement. The group itself is bringing its vision to birth.

As the first on the scene, the layer-out would often confirm the death and then prepare the body for the undertaker, enabling the family to make their appropriate farewells. The leader may have to do the same:

> When I arrived in the benefice I found it had been decided that Grinsdale church should close. It had closed during the foot and mouth outbreak and never re-opened. I felt it was important to have a final service, and managed to persuade them to re-open for one last time. There has been Christian worship there since about AD 1100. The church was full for that last communion service and at the end I led everyone out of the door and closed it behind us. With the congregation looking back over the fields to the village, I asked them to join me in a prayer of blessing on the parish. People were glad we had held that last service. It wasn't the end of their grief, but the goodbyes had been managed and people felt better for that.

ısion

A summary of the seven models of rural leadership:

- The farmer ensures health and growth.
- The entrepreneur initiates change and progress.
- The storyteller forms meaning and identity.
- The carpenter shapes and enhances what is given.
- The parent deepens love and maturity.
- The weaver draws together relationships and networks.
- The midwife / layer-out enables the transitions of life and death.

A summary of the special skills and qualities needed for rural leadership:

- An interest in and knowledge of the work, life and values of rural contexts.
- An ability to use a range of leadership and ministry styles in different churches.
- Not needing to dominate, control, or be a large fish in a small pond.
- Skills of team leadership, building collaboration and partnership, ecumenical sensitivity and co-operation.
- Creating confidence, affirming, training and equipping lay leaders. Discerning people's gifts and enabling them to exercise a spiritual ministry.
- Listening, communicating and evolving a unity of vision within complex but scattered rural networks.
- Entrepreneurial and optimistic, taking the long-term view, being patient and working at an appropriate pace.
- Developing good relationships and trust.
- Integrity, holiness, openness and transparency of life, because there is no anonymity in the countryside.
- Discretion and strict confidentiality, as people are likely to know each other.

Beyond the church?

Many secular organizations and businesses are seeking to develop leadership that is more corporate and relational, because they sense that it is effective. The models of rural leadership described are all vibrantly relational and corporate. They are lived out daily by hundreds of committed clergy and lay leaders, whose rich experience could very usefully be drawn upon by secular organizations, particularly those that operate in the countryside.

Questions

1 Which of the models of leadership are most appropriate for your context? Which do you, or could you, use yourself? Can you see ways in which the models are used by other leaders within your churches?

2 Which of the skills and qualities needed for rural leadership do you have yourself? Are there any you want to pray for, practise and develop? Which do you recognize in other leaders within your churches?

3 How could you enable other people to develop as leaders, so that rural churches can grow?

Notes

1 Alan Smith, *God-shaped Mission: Theological and Practical Perspectives from the Rural Church*, Norwich: Canterbury Press, 2008, pp. 43ff.

2 Alastair L. J. Redfern, 'Listening to the Anglican tradition', in Jeremy Martineau, Leslie J. Francis and Peter Francis (eds), *Changing Rural Life: A Christian Response to Key Rural Issues*, Norwich: Canterbury Press, 2004, p. 236.

3 Walter Brueggemann, *The Land*, London: SPCK, 1978.

4 David Jenkins, 'Has God stopped?', in John Adair and John Nelson (eds), *Creative Church Leadership*, Norwich: Canterbury Press, 2004, pp. 177 and 184.

5 Vincent Donovan, *Christianity Rediscovered*, London: SCM Press, 1982.

6 'Your Shape for God's Service'. Materials for six sessions for church groups, to help people discern their gifts for God's service. It is designed to be appropriate for all kinds of churches, including small ones. The materials are offered in a simple and flexible form so that they can be tailored and adapted to suit the context. There are no copyright restrictions. For more information, see http://www.carlislediocese.org. uk/ministry-and-vocation/everyday-life/Shape.html (accessed 3 March 2009).

7 Daniel Goleman, *Emotional Intelligence: Why It Can Matter More Than IQ*, London: Bloomsbury Publishing, 1996.

8 For more information, see Stewart C. Zabriskie, *Total Ministry*, Herndon, Virginia: The Alban Institute, 1995; Kevin L. Thew Forrester, *I Have Called You Friends . . . An Invitation to Ministry*, New York: Church Publishing, 2003; Robin Greenwood and Caroline Pascoe (eds), *Local Ministry: Story, Process and Meaning*, London: SPCK, 2006.

9 W. Bion, *Experiences in Groups*, London: Tavistock Publications, 1961.

10 Phil Kirk, 'Leadership', in Robin Greenwood and Caroline Pascoe (eds), *Local Ministry: Story, Process and Meaning*, London: SPCK, 2006, pp. 122–3.

11 Kirk, 'Leadership', p. 125.

12 Ian K. Williams, 'Enabling collaborative ministry in rural Anglicanism', *Rural Theology*, 2(2), Issue 63, 2004, pp. 89–103.

13 Simon P. Walker, *Leading Out of Who You Are: Discovering the Secret of Undefended Leadership*, Carlisle: Piquant Editions, 2007.

14 See 2 Timothy and 1 Corinthians 15.3.

15 Jim Mynors, *Pauline Perspectives*, 2006, personal communication.

16 1 Peter 2.5–9.

17 John P. Kotter, 'Leading change: why transformation efforts fail', *The Harvard Business Review*, March/April, 1995.

18 Edwin H. Friedman, *Generation to Generation*, New York: The Guilford Press, 1985.

19 Hugh Burgess, *Church Leadership in the New Millennium*, Porvoo Communion Church Leaders' Consultation, 2002.

20 Russ Parker, *Healing Wounded History*, London: Darton, Longman and Todd, 2001.

21 For a full discussion, see E. H. Friedman, *Generation to Generation*, New York: The Guilford Press, 1985; R. W. Richardson, *Creating a Healthier Church: Family Systems Theory, Leadership and Congregational Life*, Minneapolis: Fortress Press, 1996; P. L. Steinke, *How Your Church Family Works*, Herndon, Virginia: The Alban Institute, 1993.

22 Philippians 2.1–11.

I want to thank the following people, who are all engaged in rural leadership, for their contributions to this chapter through helpful discussions and sending me ideas, quotations and stories: the Rt Revd Graham Dow, the Rt Revd James Newcome, and the Revds Gill Hart, Beth Smith, Colin Randall, Colin Honour, Roger Latham, Jonathan Falkner, Stephen Walker, Tim Evans, and Nigel Davies.

4

Pastoral ministry

LESLIE MORLEY AND
DAGMAR WINTER

Specific aspects of pastoral ministry in the countryside, its opportunities, its peculiarities and its challenges are discussed in this chapter. The first part sets out pastorally significant issues in rural Britain today, and the second describes the varied forms of pastoral response required by this context and affirms the pastoral role of the church within rural community life.

Introduction

In the last two decades, rural communities have been marked by significant change. The church, in terms of both the building and congregation, still has a presence in almost every rural community, even if the paid minister is not resident there. Thus the church has a crucial role to play in supporting communities and individuals as they face the implications of change in rural life. This presents new opportunities and challenges for pastoral ministry.

The Rural Context and its Pastoral Significance

Geography and history

The geography of an area will profoundly shape the communities living there. It will also interplay with its military, economic, industrial, sociological and agricultural history. While 'rural' implies areas less densely populated, there are nevertheless significant differences between those areas that are sparsely populated and those with larger populations. Evidence suggests that in sparsely populated communities people are more involved in local groups and networks and are therefore more accessible for pastoral care, whereas in more populous communities life may be more fragmented, and hence more difficult to access for the pastor.

Demography

One of the most significant factors reshaping rural communities is the changing demographic profile of the countryside. There are particular pastoral issues associated with: an ageing population, the inward migration of predominantly wealthy younger families, the absence of young adults (aged 15–24) and, in some communities, an increasing number of migrant workers.

These demographic changes lead to a resident community that is rarely homogenous. There are clear pastoral implications as differing expectations of the countryside, and differing levels of access to economic and social goods, may become a source of tension between the indigenous population and those moving from urban areas to the countryside. Those exercising pastoral ministry therefore need to provide opportunities for mutual understanding and co-operation to serve the common good.

There are particular issues around young people since youth culture remains largely invisible in rural areas. This presents the church with the pastoral challenge of supporting young people in their search for the company of others with whom they can shape a space for themselves.

The proportion of the rural population under the age of 15 – at 15% – is the same as that for the urban population and yet, because their numbers are small, they are less visible and their needs may be neglected. The lack of public transport limits the activities and opportunities available for young people in the countryside. These include access to youth services and advice centres catering to young people's needs, after-school activities, places for meeting and entertainment. This can lead to young people growing up with limited horizons and aspirations. The church's ecumenical, deanery and diocesan networks can provide the context in which young people can come together, find support and participate in a wider social framework.

The exodus of young adults from rural communities, who leave to further their education, to find employment and access affordable housing, has an impact on traditional patterns of care within families and among neighbours. As the rural population ages, it will mean there will be more sick and housebound people, and greater isolation for those whose younger family members have had to move away. This will be a challenge to the churches and make greater demands on pastoral resources. In turn, evidence suggests that older people are more likely to engage in voluntary activities than younger people, and therefore may also be a resource for the church's pastoral response to these growing needs.

Disadvantage

One in five rural households live below the official poverty line, but the dispersed nature of rural disadvantage means that it is often hidden from view. Disadvantage is further hidden by a culture of self-reliance and pride that makes rural people reluctant to seek help and admit to need. It can also be difficult to seek help in rural communities as there is, on the one hand, a lack of anonymity and, on the other, few support agencies that are easily accessible. Those exercising pastoral ministry in such circumstances need to be aware of the factors inhibiting access to personal support, and to be particularly discerning and sensitive in their approach.[1]

The loss of key services in rural communities, such as transport links, the village shop, the pub and the post office, alongside the threat to the survival of small village schools, reduces the opportunities for people to meet, share information and offer mutual support, further re-enforcing social isolation. Where these remain, they continue to be places where people access pastoral support and where information is exchanged about the needs of others. The challenge to the church is how it can be a focus for community gatherings and support the networks of informal care where these are growing more fragile.

Access poverty (poor transport services reducing the ease of access to vital services) has a very direct and distressing effect on rural health; this is called 'distance-decay'. This means that the further away patients are from hospitals, the less likely they are to seek the attention of a GP.[2] The importance of travel in order to access work, education, any necessary service or social life, highlights the problem of isolation in rural communities. These problems are obvious for those who are housebound, who require visiting and care both by professionals and by neighbours and family. But isolation and difficulties of access are acute issues for those who have no private transport due to their youth, their old age or their inability to afford a car – often the so-called 'indigenous poor'. Pastoral care here may mean becoming involved with practical solutions such as a community shop and post office or a shared transport scheme.

The lack of affordable housing and of accommodation for rent continues to be one of the most pressing problems facing many rural families who cannot afford to live in the local communities to which they belong. Pastoral skill is needed to overcome resistance to sensitive affordable developments within a village from those wanting only to preserve what is there already.

Those disadvantaged include not only those who suffer material deprivation. Indeed, those who are poor share with other groups a further disadvantage, which is invisibility. Invariably, given the small numbers in a rural setting, issues and problems fall below the radar of government or local authority statistics, which means that appropriate services and resources are not allocated appropriately. Young people or migrant workers in particular fall into this category. Recognizing the less visible is an important pastoral skill in this context.

Farming

Though rural communities are in a state of flux, farming remains both critical and essential to their existence. Increased mechanization and poor economic returns have led to serious levels of stress and isolation for many farmers and farming families. Long working hours, unpredictable weather, volatile prices, and the lack of separation between work and domestic life are all sources of stress for farmers. Often a farm will have been in the family for a number of generations. This increases the pressure on those who, in difficult times, feel a particular responsibility to past generations to continue farming beyond economic viability. Response by the churches in day-to-day pastoral care, and also in addressing crises, is vital.

The outbreak of foot and mouth during 2001 acted as a stark reminder of the importance of the presence of effective pastoral response within every rural community. It is significant that the church was not regarded as an external emergency service addressing short-term needs, but as a part of a community that was living through devastating suffering. It shared the immediate trauma of the events and was therefore also able to be an authentic sign of continuity and hope.

Migrant workers

The influx of migrant workers, some seasonal and others in permanent jobs on farms, in food processing and tourism, has placed new demands on rural services. The culture and faith of migrant workers from the EU countries may enrich local life or be perceived as a threat, and relating to them can be a particular pastoral opportunity for working with whole communities rather than with individuals alone. In response to the migrants' presence, churches have offered hospitality, enabling newcomers to find their way into the local community and to also find acceptance. They have provided information on rights and services, as well as being a source of spiritual support. Where employment practice is poor and exploitative, the pastoral work of the church will be clearly linked with its advocacy and prophetic role, drawing attention to grievances: 'Pastoral care takes seriously the social and political context of care . . . its ultimate aim being not merely adjustment to, but the transformation of, society.'[3]

Extended parishioners

The term 'extended parishioners' has been used to describe those people who no longer live in a particular rural parish, or indeed may never have done so, but whose connections with the place, through their families, their work, or through the local school, are such that they seek the ministry of that church at critical moments of their lives, for celebrations or for solace.[4] These connections offer opportunities for significant pastoral encounters, though they also raise pastorally sensitive questions about the use of time, and respect for parochial boundaries. Many rural churches also find themselves offering an anonymous pastoral ministry to tourists and visitors to the church building. This is through the literature provided for visitors, and through opportunities to offer or ask for prayers by lighting candles or filling out prayer requests. In busy centres of tourism some churches provide a rota of people offering a ministry of welcome. These are forms of extended pastoral ministry at the heart of which is a ministry of hospitality, which reflects the gracious hospitality of God.

The Pastoral Response

The essence of pastoral ministry in the rural context

We understand pastoral ministry as God's loving care extended to all people, not just to church members, in which Christ's promise of life in all its fullness is offered to communities as well as to individuals, in daily life, in happy and in sad times. The resources of the Christian faith to understand, interpret and manage the changes that rural communities are undergoing are part of this offering. Such pastoral care will always be offered in the context of, and together with, the whole Christian community. Often as a result of this pastoral engagement, the church will find its prophetic voice.

Structured listening as a basic requirement

In order to facilitate pastoral ministry, structured listening to the individual and the community is essential. It requires an openness to expressions of points of view or feelings with which the pastor may or may not be comfortable, hence appropriate self-awareness is a prerequisite to effective listening. Structured listening at the beginning of ministry in a particular location is the basis for any future pastoral work and, indeed, ministry in general. Such listening will include a friendly inquisitiveness which draws out people's delight in sharing stories of themselves, their family and community. Especially when arriving as a newcomer, being prepared to admit to knowing next to nothing about local people, their life, history and work, will open many doors and lead to many helpful encounters. Searching people out at home, at work, or at other gathering places is an authentic expression of valuing people and their lives, which lies at the heart of the incarnation. Structured listening also helps the minister to remember, which is an equally important aspect of pastoral ministry. The pastor who can recall the story of the community, its families and individuals demonstrates his or her sense of belonging to that community. Memory is also a vital element in the process of coping with and managing change in the life of individuals and communities. A pastor who can help people access their own memories in times of crisis directs them towards sources of hope.

Working with existing pastoral structures

Audit

The first step in any plan for church engagement should always be an audit of existing forms of pastoral care and listening. Partnership working must mean that churches do not seek to take over or monopolize the good pastoral care that happens beyond their immediate sphere of influence. Strengthening community life does not mean strengthening one particular group identity, but strengthening a sense of awareness and openness for one another, within and across these groupings.

Informal structures and networks

Identifying and entering into the natural centres of communication is an obvious thing to do. The chat, news and gossip that are exchanged at the school gate, in the post office, the village shop, the pub, at the livestock Mart and in the church, not only indicate the state of health of the individual, but also express something about the health of the community. These opportunities give access to differing age groups and social networks, some of which may be dysfunctional, whereas others may be extremely positive and helpful. People may be included and cared for or excluded and disregarded. The phrase of 'gossiping the gospel' can gain new meaning when the pastor engages with compassion in these conversations.

Those institutions within a rural community that exist for a particular purpose – for example, the sports club – will also offer opportunity for informal pastoral support. Partnership here can mean either learning from, joining, supporting and strengthening those people and informal structures that do good work, or looking at the reasons for destructive dynamics and addressing and challenging them.

The strength of knowing each other well, good neighbourliness and gossip, with the corresponding lack of anonymity, are both a blessing and a curse. The problem of disclosure of private or personal matters within tight-knit communities cannot be overestimated. The rural pastor needs to be particularly sensitive to issues of confidentiality and disclosure, particularly when coming from a background where such issues might have been shared within a ministry team.

Structured support networks

The pastor living in a rural community needs to work with the statutory and voluntary agencies involved in the benefice. This will often mean looking beyond benefice boundaries to where these organizations are based. Structured support networks include special interest groups such as the Women's Institute, the British Legion, Young Farmers, sports clubs, youth / children / toddler clubs, schools and associated groups, village hall committees, the parish council and other community action groups. Local GP surgeries and other health practitioners – especially community nurses, advice centres, often covering a larger area, and those who bring services to people's homes – are all highly significant players in supporting community life, particularly for those who are vulnerable. For a successful partnership, churches and other service providers need to be open with one another about their underlying values and intentions.[5]

While web-based support (for example, for those suffering from particular illnesses) and virtual blogging communities may be more difficult for the pastor to associate with due to their invisibility, nevertheless they offer invaluable support to some rural residents.

The value of networks of pastoral support beyond the parish was evident during disease outbreaks affecting agriculture in recent years. Advice and support from the Farming Help

Partnership of Farm Crisis Network, the Royal Agricultural Benevolent Institution and the ARC-Addington Fund, enabled the churches to make an effective and co-ordinated response, offering practical help alongside informed prayerful support. Awareness of these and other local networks is essential for the pastoral ministry of the rural church.

Alongside the statutory and voluntary agencies, it is also important to note those support structures that are directly facilitated by the church: the Mothers' Union, pastoral groups, bereavement visitors, midweek coffee mornings and lunch clubs, and other groups for people of a particular age or gender, as well as home groups and, of course, the occasional offices that speak into people's lives. These are all often underrated contributions with which the church supports individuals and the fabric of community life.

A word of warning about the church's pastoral work: one of the dangers of official pastoral groups offering a visiting service or similar is that they can be seen to clericalize or professionalize the neighbourliness and milk of human kindness that people offer one to the other. This disables its essentially informal expression. Pastoral groups should honour any other good work that goes on in the community, just as they need to honour the strength and pride that people display. Misguided forms of pastoral work can create dependency rather than strengthening people to tackle the issues themselves with which they need to deal.

Given the nature of rural communities and the thankfully much lower thresholds between denominations, ecumenical co-operation in any pastoral work is imperative.

In this way, pastoral groups work organically with the nature of rural community and also provide a good living example of community co-operation for the benefit of all. All too often, particularly in more traditional settings, the churches' contributions are focused on the clergy. Being less collaborative and more directive than he or she originally set out to be is a huge temptation in small communities and needs to be recognized and resisted.

Good practice includes not only supervision of colleagues, but also regular meetings – for example, between ministers of different denominations – in order to exchange observations and concerns and to co-ordinate any action. Such a supportive network can also be a considerable help in dealing with the high level of expectation and corresponding pressure from which the professional pastors suffer in the countryside.

Church and community

For most people the quality of their lives is connected to their sense of belonging and of being valued within a particular location. This location may relate to networks of shared interest and experiences but for many, particularly in the countryside, it is still related to a sense of place, and to participation within a local community. Strengthening community life is a vital aspect of pastoral work. In those urban or suburban areas with few bonds among people in a locality, helping to create a sense of community becomes a very important contribution of the church. The church is then often the generator of community action programmes of support and care in the wider community.

By contrast, many rural settlements already have a strong sense of community (more likely several). The church's role therefore in celebrating such an existing sense of community will be different from that in a suburban area. It would be counterproductive for the church to seek to establish itself as an alternative community. Instead, the contributions that individual church members make to the wider community needs to be valued. Two recent studies, *Faith in Rural Communities* (2006)[6] and *Faith in the Community* (2007),[7] have shown that church members are well represented in voluntary activities which fundamentally support rural community life.

The support of the church for community events and occasions is a visible expression of its care and concern at the heart of community life. This is a role shared by both clergy and laity, each of whom have significant but distinctive roles as part of that visible presence. Although in a multi-parish benefice clergy can feel stretched in making themselves visible and available, the impact of being at just some of the significant moments and events in a village can be out of all proportion to the amount of time invested. A presence at, for example, the local country show or village fête can provide an opportunity to meet people and be known (and assessed) and may lead to deeper pastoral relationships. It will also be a representative presence indicating the church's concern for the well-being not just of its own institutional life, but of the wider community, and showing a desire to share in its celebrations. In this way clergy in multi-parish benefices are able to demonstrate their commitment to, and involvement with, the various communities they serve, even though they cannot be at everything. Discerning critical opportunities of engagement is an essential skill.

Visibility is, however, not limited to the role of the clergy. A high proportion of church members involve themselves in village activities in a way that is often unacknowledged, even by the church. It is surprising, and regrettable, how rarely members of a congregation are prayed for in the intercessions in rural churches in their roles or work within the community, as parish councillors, on the village hall or show committee, or in caring for their neighbours. They also are the visible face of the church in the community and those who have a lay ministerial position may find themselves drawn into pastoral situations through the relationships they develop in their roles within that wider community. They too represent the church, and demonstrate in practical ways the pastoral agency of the local church. In many villages a key member of the congregation, perhaps from a long-established indigenous family, comes to be regarded by many as the person who in some way embodies the life and values of the church. That person may have no formal role, but carries for others what the church is for, and is the person people speak to when they seek the church's ministry or support. It is important in pastoral ministry to know and work with the person the community identifies as its link to the church.

The church will only reach its full pastoral potential when the authorized minister and church members live and work as reflective practitioners, sharing insight and learning from one another.

Finally, it is important to note that pastoral care and its visibility, not least in rural communities, has at least as much to do with being as with doing. In the rural context, who you are as a person matters as much as what you do. Rural communities can know their clergy in a way that is less feasible in an urban context, and so come to value the depth and integrity of their clergy more than their activism. Holding that 'being' in the intensity of rural community living can be a formidable task in itself indeed and the power of presence should not be underestimated. During the foot and mouth outbreak in 2001, the ministry of the church was effective and credible in part because it was a ministry from within the community, of people known and trusted.

Occasional offices and seasonal services

The nature of rural social networks, and of extended family ties, means that the occasional offices take on a communal dimension rather than being confined to the immediate families of those involved. This is especially true of village funerals. Where funerals in an urban context are more often than not private occasions for family and friends, in the countryside they are more typically public occasions involving the wider community. At these times pastoral ministry will be to the whole community as well as to those immediately bereaved. The service will need to articulate the feelings of the whole community and provide a liturgical context for expressing both grief and hope. Many a new rural priest has discovered that their first village funeral was key to their acceptance, or otherwise, by the village.

There are many opportunities during the year to affirm various sections of the community, as well as uniting the community as a whole, through the rediscovery of communal rites and celebrations. The agricultural year provides occasions to express care and concern for the well-being of the farming community through demonstrating awareness of the circumstances affecting farmers, and by giving events in the agricultural calendar a place in the life of the church and in that of the wider community. There are opportunities here for creative worship and celebrations. Harvest thanksgivings, rogation services and lambing services are increasingly held on farms, with special invitations sent to farmers and the local community, drawing in the resources of the local band, school and other village organizations.

Special times of the church's year, such as All Souls' Day and Remembrance Sunday, provide opportunities for collective participation and remembering, as do highlights of the school year celebrated in an act of worship. Christmas and Easter have been the focus for street drama in some villages, with the nativity or the passion story anchored in the life of the local community, providing an opportunity for people to participate and identify with the key events of the gospel. In the rural context, worship offers a way of ministering to a whole community, and for the community to come together in a spiritual environment. *Common Worship: Times and Seasons* offers a rich resource for such celebrations, including material for the agricultural year.[8]

Church and churchyard

In the countryside, a sense of place and belonging is often associated with the symbolic value of the church building, which can offer an awareness of history and continuity. The building is a focus for the story or social history of the village, giving a sense of belonging to a community that has existed through time. It also represents, in its continued pattern of regular worship, community celebrations and pastoral offices, the importance of the transcendent in the life of a sustainable and sustaining community. For some, facing the challenges of a changing countryside, the church building may therefore come to represent an unchanging but mythical past and a refuge from the present and future. However, the church, when its story is unfolded, represents both continuity and change. The building is in fact a witness to the many changes and upheavals that have faced a particular community throughout its story. It has the possibility, therefore, when interpreted, to encourage a creative rather than a defensive response to the profound challenges currently facing both rural churches and rural communities.

An important extended part of the church building is its churchyard and often also its war memorial. The church is here invested with a high level of trust and is respected as holding the treasured vestiges of the community's history. Correspondingly, any changes that might affect either church or graveyard – such as internal reordering, the building of an annexe, conversion to an eco-churchyard, and the introduction of mobile telephone masts – are pastorally hugely sensitive. Mishandled, such issues can turn into a pastoral disaster undermining much previous work and creating difficulties for future work. In turn, dealing with such issues thoughtfully will be understood as a clear signal that the community, its history and, by inference, its individuals and their feelings, are valued.

Conclusion

The church's long-term commitment to the countryside stands in contrast to many projects which, due to the nature of funding in the voluntary sector, are short term. This affords the church an opportunity to build long-term relationships, respect and credibility. Where the resources for pastoral support are changing, from being focused exclusively on the full-time ordained person towards lay pastoral teams supported by clergy, it is important for the clergy to be in post long enough to establish new patterns of ministry. In addition, they must manage the expectations, of both church and the community, of the role of ordained ministry and of the incumbent in particular. Pastoral developments involving lay teams need to be supported and developed by successive incumbents, and appointing authorities need to guard against the good work of one incumbent being overturned by the successor.

Integral to pastoral care is the ability to engage in theological reflection, for pastoral care involves helping people and communities both to explore and to discover meaning within the events that affect and change their lives. Pastoral care is about helping people and communities manage change in response to a God of resurrection who transforms our fears by drawing us into his kingdom of grace and love.

At a time when the countryside is experiencing something of a paradigm shift in its way of life, it is important that pastors can offer theological resources and theological leadership that enables people to work with, or to challenge, these changes. And if the church is to fulfil its role in the wider national context it also needs an informed prophetic voice to address the issues facing the countryside. Despite efforts of rural proofing and rural mainstreaming, government structures and support still have an urban bias and the church itself in its strategic planning is only now gradually becoming more aware of rural issues.

The countryside is currently the focus of many of the crucial issues facing our society and culture: the contested use of land for leisure, food or biofuel production, the preservation of biodiversity; the nature of community and its sustainability; the impact of globalization; the integration of new migrants. Far from being the gentle backdrop to dynamic urban life, the countryside is a laboratory where complex issues vital to the future of society are being worked out. In engaging pastorally and theologically with these concerns, the church finds itself at the heart of the current agenda.

Questions

1 What are the main opportunities and the main difficulties for pastoral ministry in the countryside in your context?

2 How do you see pastoral ministry relating to different sections of a rural community?

3 How would you describe the future challenges facing pastoral ministry in a changing church and countryside?

Notes

1 See also the section 'Informal structures and networks', p. 87, for a discussion on the lack of anonymity as both a positive and a negative, and for the heightened importance of confidentiality.

2 Iain J. Mungall, *Ensuring Equitable Access to Health and Social Care for Rural and Remote Communities. Increasing Centralisation and Specialisation within the NHS: The Trend has Some Adverse Effects on Access to Care for Rural and Remote Communities*, pp. 2–4, http://www.rural-health.ac.uk/publications/mungall-equitable-access.pdf (accessed 27 March 2009).

3 David Lyall, *Integrity of Pastoral Care*, London: SPCK, 2001, p. 12.

4 Martin Coppen, 'The extended parish', *Rural Theology*, 3(2), Issue 65, 2005, pp. 99–111.

5 A good answer is offered by *Faith in the Countryside*: 'It is part of our response to God to create conditions where others in community can experience care and well-being. For the Church to be truly committed to enabling persons to grow will involve the task of ensuring that society is organised in such a way that human beings can enter freely into these relationships of spiritual and material exchange that we call loving relationships' (Archbishops' Commission on Rural Areas, *Faith in the Countryside*, Worthing: Churchman Publishing, 1990, pp. 22–3).

6 R. Farnell, J. Hopkinson, D. Jarvis, J. Martineau and J. Ricketts Hein, *Faith in Rural Communities: Contributions of Social Capital to Community Vibrancy*, Stoneleigh Park: Acora Publishing, 2006.

7 J. Grieve, V. Jochum, B. Pratten and C. Steel, *Faith in the Community: The Contribution of Faith-based Organisations to Rural Voluntary Action*, London: NCVO, 2007.

8 Church of England, *Common Worship: Times and Seasons*, London: Church House Publishing, 2006.

5

Encouraging vocational pathways

MARK SANDERS

In this chapter I want to affirm the growing diversity of vocational expression in rural parishes. This involves exploring how God's mission is shaping the church and the call of individuals within rural settings, and this leads me to challenge some common assumptions about vocation and church.

The first assumption to be challenged is that vocation is only God's call to those who wish to be ordained. Theologies of mission and ministry challenge us to look beyond narrow definitions. The life and needs of the modern rural church give different examples of how vocation is being worked out and indicates what still needs to be done to encourage it further.

Mission, ministry and vocation

'It is not the Church of God that has a mission in the world, but the God of mission who has a Church in the world.'[1] Creation, redemption and inspiration are the outpouring of God's trinitarian love for humanity and the universe. The life of the church originates in this outpouring and so is necessarily involved in proclaiming the gospel, in tending to those in need, active in the cause of justice and aware of the needs of creation. Rural ministry does this through involvement with socially diverse communities within a small area and where surrounding fields raise issues of environment, world food supply and the use of modern technology. The formation of the church as community happens through the preaching of the word and the celebration of the sacraments and attempts to embody the love of the Trinity within such contexts. And the church tries to be 'not as a homogenous unity but as a differentiated oneness of distinctive persons-in-relation who discover their particularity in active relationships of giving and receiving'.[2]

Vocation has often been understood as a definite and distinct calling of individuals into church roles. However, this does not reflect the tentative and mysterious vocational experience of many who explore ordination. And this understanding is exploded by the trinitarian theology of mission which results in richer views of vocation. Vocation is the activity of God shaping his church, that it might be fit to participate in his mission. This allows for the development of a view that sees how the Spirit calls people into distinctive, varying and complementary roles within and beyond the church as part of God's outpouring of love for the whole of creation.

Paul sees the church as the body of Christ formed of people with differing gifts being exercised to build up others.[3] These passages seem to focus on people called to serve the church. Given he was writing to new churches in the act of forming, this is not surprising. In the Petrine epistles the early church communities are seen as exiles or resident aliens relating with difficulty to their society and culture.[4] Their call to holy living is individually and corporately to proclaim the message of how to be Christ-like, and so proclaim Christ in deed as well as word. Holiness codes for behaviour within families were an expression of this.[5] Being Christian is to be richly and newly human and our discipleship is to pattern us according to the example of Jesus Christ.

In the Gospels we have many stories of people responding to Jesus' call to follow him. The choosing of the twelve apostles might be seen as the classic call, but theologies of ministry are divided as to whether this is the call of the first disciples and so the pattern for all discipleship, or the call of the first representative ministry for the church.

The thread running through this is that call leads to response: vocation is not an end in itself, but continues to be expressed through prayer and action. Furthermore, the sense that all Christians have a vocation and ministry is now commonly accepted. The World Council of Churches' Lima text, *Baptism, Eucharist and Ministry*, suggests:

> The Holy Spirit bestows on the community diverse and complementary gifts. These are for the common good of the whole people and are manifested in acts of service within the community and to the world . . . for the building up of the Church and for the service of the world to which the Church is sent.[6]

From rural America:

> Vocation is the response to inspiration . . . It leads us to promise to be part of a God-centred company that lives in grace . . . Vocation is then our acceptance of the Spirit's co-ordination of our gifts, and the Spirit provides the energy, the momentum and the context . . . whether that be work-place, home, school or play environments.[7]

In both quotes there is an interplay of gifts given to individuals and the building up of the church in mission.

The call leads us to respond to God's mission to the whole world and not solely to the community of the church. Mission and ministry are thus the response of the whole people of God to God's continuing, loving acts in his world. Reports such as *All Are Called* stressed that God's call is for all the laity as well as the clergy. It is for the laos' 'churchly ministries' for 'our ministries with family, friends and neighbours . . . for what have been called our "Monday morning" ministries . . . and for our "Saturday night" ministries'.[8]

Some writers make a sharper distinction between ministry and discipleship and there is a danger that broadening the ideas of ministry or vocation leads them to mean almost everything! In terms of vocation, the distinction is expressed by some being called to have a particular role in shaping and leading the people of God. This role, be it ordained or authorized lay (reader or other recognized lay roles), is not more important or qualitatively different than other roles. Rather, it is part of the dynamism of community being expressed in the particularity of gifts needed to keep the church true to its role within God's mission and thus true to itself. A trinitarian theology stresses that vocation, mission and the church are formed by the grace and love of God acting on all who would call themselves Christians. People are called to specific roles and relationships within the church. This needs to be seen within the same call of God for all his church through the particularity of gifts and their shaping by the Spirit within community.

What are the telltale signs that this might be happening? First, that people who have no intention of being ordained or becoming readers, and may not naturally use vocational language, still seem to be consciously and deliberately engaging with a sense that God has given them gifts to serve others and to serve the church.

This leads to a second point, that the encouraging of such a vocational understanding may disrupt the traditional Anglican pattern that the incumbent does ministry vicariously for the church. So a telltale sign of a dynamic understanding of vocation is an increase in the whole church being able to say what it is about. This will be expressed in collaborative ministry and a growing ability to make use of gifts in response to a sense of vocation. More authorized ministers will not just keep the show on the road, but through their differing gifts and experiences broaden the horizon of the church and its activities. Collaborative ministry, ministry teams and ecumenical partnerships should be modelling shared ministry, encouraging and equipping congregations to see that mission and ministry is not the task of an individual. That means mission and ministry is open to all and not restricted by age or gender.

Third, this does not deny the need for authorized ministry, but it does change the way it may need to be exercised. Instead of doing ministry on behalf of others, alongside their public representative role, authorized ministers are likely to be the animator as well as the practitioner of ministry. This may mean a change both within the perception of the vocation of the ordained and of the expectation of some congregations.

I would not see these three signs as exclusively rural. But part of the work behind this chapter was a number of conversations across a rural diocese about whether there is anything distinctively rural about vocation and ministry. Views varied, but several PCCs and groups talked about 'you can't hide in a rural parish', 'you know your neighbours', 'we have to encounter difference'. These comments have differing vocational consequences. On the one hand, people may be reluctant to 'push themselves forward' and take up positions of leadership. But on the other hand, where there is encouragement as well as knowledge of how people's gifts are used within the community, people may find themselves almost pushed to the fore. Cathy – an ordained local minister, whose story is mentioned later – is a case of this.

In a rural setting it is hard just to attend church. In a wider society where it is not the norm to worship and actively belong to a church, to use one's gifts in the name of God is to make a visible faith commitment. This can be questioned or applauded. Doing something explicitly linked with the faith of the church is a very public act in a village. Instinctive Anglican reticence may be under threat!

On the other hand, the church building is still a central focus providing continuity and inspiring loyalty, even from non-attenders who may become involved in 'Friends of the Church' and organize social events. This promotes community, which is important too, in that relationships and knowledge of people form a sense of belonging. This may be to buy into a rural myth, and undoubtedly some residents now use villages as dormitories from which they travel out to work or leisure, but compared to the urban or suburban there is a smallness of scale that increases the possibility of relationships in the locality. This can create fuzzy edges between the church and its locality, especially in some of the ways people are involved with the church. Some have an association with the church without being worshippers or even believers.

Does this mean that people doing the flowers, ringing the bells or mowing the churchyard are, as some do say, participating in ministry? Some of these things are done as an expression of faith, but the bellringers who do not worship may not want to be considered as Christians – let alone ministers. The man who mows may be glad to do so because he has family in the churchyard, but have no wish for this to be seen as an act of faith. They may see it as something they are willing to offer, but is this vocation or ministry or good will? Perhaps the dilemma is greater in rural settings. Because of the network of relationships, the place of the building, possible personal knowledge of the incumbent or other minister, it is easier for those with little faith (or none) to be involved in the life of the church, which in an urban setting is increasingly a matter of deliberate choice. How a loose association with the church can be used to help people explore faith is an opportunity for all churches, but perhaps especially the rural church. But such association is perhaps not best interpreted as a vocation or ministry.

The following story demonstrates both a lay person exploring the use of her gifts in mission and someone who struggles with the vocational language that could be used to describe it. It also suggests some of the fuzziness of boundaries between church and community. The church encourages her and gives her a forum to work with young parents; her work is part of a pastoral outreach to many who would not otherwise go to church to worship.

This is the story of Liz:

Liz had been a nurse, which she expressed as a vocation. While a health visitor, she had developed an interest in infant massage which builds on the parent's instinct to hold and stroke. When she finished her employment she used this at a church 'Tiddlers and Toddlers' group and in the local church primary school. This has allowed deep conversations to go on, not just about the children, but also about the stresses and joys of parenting and what the church is about. I was keen to make links between this and mission, ministry and vocation. However, Liz was reluctant to use vocational language about her work with massage, even though she mentioned conversations about suffering, pain and forming relationships not only between people, but also between people and the church. She recognized how the vicar and church had encouraged and authorized this work in the village for wider acceptability, but there was a firm sense that her massage work was about her humanity and love of people, rather than something she wished to see labelled as vocation or ministry.

Liz's reaction was a surprise, and I am not sure that I got to the root of it. Perhaps it was a natural humility; probably it had something to do with the fact that vocation is seen as a divine call to church ministry, especially ordination, in contrast to what people experience as arising out of the normal interaction and relations of rural life.

What Liz is doing could now be labelled as a potential 'Fresh Expression of church' and if parents within the group sought baptism for themselves or the children, such an approach would ask whether their church would be the 'Tiddlers and Toddlers' group or the Sunday congregation. The teaching around what it is to be church in mission, and the role and vocation of members to be engaged and involved, are important counterbalances to traditional models of going to church and of a parson who does ministry on behalf of the church. Taking seriously teaching about vocation means to make definite connections between the gifts people bring and how those gifts form or challenge what is seen as church and mission activities.

The reluctance of rural church-goers who regularly visit others to claim a vocation or a labelled ministry has been frequently commented on and relates to the nature of rural community. Sometimes visiting is done by people explicitly as members of the church, but often not, and when asked to consider a formal ministry they say that such ministries are for more important people. Or it is felt that labels can get in the way of relationships between people in a village. It would be as if to place yourself above someone else, which would harm the relationships that are so important. So their intention is to be a good neighbour rather than a representative minister. This idea has caused dispute among diocesan officers. Some say that connections between action and faith are readily made; others that it is simply the quality of human care that motivates people, though this could also be seen as the work of God. It is my experience that some people, when asked, would not explicitly link their behaviour with vocation or their faith. This is much more the case in the country, and their links with individuals and groups are likely to be far more than just people they know from going to church. To put it differently, the pattern of relationships even within the congregation is not dependent on church-going. The existence of many interlocking patterns of relationship within a village community may mean people are resistant to taking on formal roles or claiming vocational language for their own actions.

It is also worth noting Liz's multiple roles in village and church, which is a common feature in rural communities. A disproportionate number of church members are also found on governing bodies, parish councils and running the Women's Institute, but do not always explicitly or willingly link this with their Christian vocation as disciples.

What are the roles of a diocese in vocation initiatives?

The resistance to expressing vocation needs to inform the encouragement for vocations provided by a diocese. This can be done by taking seriously the vocation and ministry of all the baptized. Vocation advisers are lay and ordained people available to all church members to discuss God's call and direction in their life, at any or many points in their lives. The Diocese of St Edmundsbury and Ipswich has developed a seven-session vocations course which explores how God calls all his people into discipleship and ministry. The course aims to help people link their lives with mission and with ideas of ministry including the possibility, but not inevitability, of authorized ministry. The continuing consultation with and reference to the vocations advisers appointed by the diocese is also encouraged. However, after one year the advisers commented that most of the people they had seen had been seeking a church-based ministry: for a few, it was reader ministry, and for the majority it was for ordained. Sadly, but perhaps not surprisingly, a vocational perspective of careers such as teaching or medicine has not been promoted through the work of the advisers, though the vocations course does explore these areas. One conclusion may be read that vocation, when promoted by a diocese, is understood to refer only to the church.

Encouragingly, on one vocational course someone decided against formal ministry and explored how to serve the local communities through training as an adviser for Citizens Advice. While exploring ordained local ministry, someone else realized how God was using her already within her role as a health visitor. Thus there needs to be more active partnership with other agencies to link volunteering in the wider community with a broader understanding of vocation.

Helping people to explore explicitly gifts and vocation is not a new challenge, but in an age when faith can be seen as an optional Sunday activity, it is needed for the integration of faith and life. The church may need to be encouraged to accept and then bless the work of its members when it draws them away from direct church-related activity. There is a sacrificial element here too for the church, as gifts and skills are used on other projects and tasks. But the needs of mission do have to be prioritized over that of keeping the church running. That is easy to say, but every incumbent faces the temptation to focus on maintenance only.

In reviewing the impact of this diocese's vocations course, questions were asked of participants: 'do you use the word "vocation" about your Christian life?' Two who are exploring authorized ministry affirmed they did. Others, all from rural benefices, replied:

- 'Not really . . . I find expressions like leading, journey, being a channel, expresses experience in my life.'
- 'No.'
- 'No, God is my guide, leader, the one who knows what is best for me, the one who has created me, given me gifts that he wants me to use.'

On a very small sample any conclusion must be tentative and open to a number of explanations, but on a positive note these comments suggest that time spent looking at a broader under-standing of vocation can help people see God's hand at work in their lives and realize their gifts. But, even so, the word 'voca-tion' is related to formal ministry by others and not to them-selves. The lay training adviser in St Edmundsbury and Ipswich diocese testifies that people are willing to make connections between God and how the church should be in relation to the communities around them, but the rich theological concepts of vocation, mission and ministry are sometimes professionalized. This needs to be countered.

Encouraging vocation as the active expression of gifts

There is a continuing need to be proactive in encouraging people to think about how we are called to use our gifts and express our discipleship. In rural communities where so much of this seems to happen as a result of naturally occurring rela-tionships as well as church-based activities, there needs to be a deliberate strategy of reminding one another that we are called to follow Christ first. The points that follow are suggestions for study courses, preaching series, diocesan initiatives, focuses for services or intercessions, to encourage a broader understanding of vocation.

- Encourage groups to work at a rich and broad understanding of vocation. Within this, no one vocation should be ranked before another; rather, they are all an outworking of the Spirit within the body of Christ. This would need to expose traditional expectations of who 'does' ministry and suggest new patterns of how ministry can be worked at together.

- Develop ways of helping rural churches explore and express gifts. For example, 'Shape', from Carlisle diocese, is a six-session course for church groups, to help people discern their gifts for God's service.[9]

- Groups could be helped to consider how the church is involved in the local community through the work of individuals, and what the church itself offers (for example, social events, rites of passage, regular worship), and how this links with an understanding of God's mission. A series of events exploring the Five Marks of Mission could be used.[10] One deanery synod used one Mark for each of their meetings over a couple of years.

- Parish audits have traditionally looked at the statutory and voluntary organizations in a village. Along with this, a PCC, study group or congregation could look at who within their number is involved with what and build up a picture of how people have multiple roles and involvement. They can be supported by prayer and intercessions and challenged to think how they are present in different places in the village, benefice or wider area on behalf of God, whether in a formal role or not. The next step is to explore how this can be recognized and celebrated as part of mission.[11]

- Rural benefices could be encouraged to release people's time to explore other activities within mission and ministry rather than recruiting people to do the many tasks needed to keep the show on the road. This could be affirmed in fostering partnerships to encourage volunteering, which could become mutual in benefit between parishes in a benefice and between communities.

What are the pathways that lead to collaborative and mission-focused authorized ministry?

At one stage, rural authorized ministry consisted of the incumbent who (hopefully) felt called to visit, to preach and to pray for the people of that place, and be involved with birth, marriages, sickness and death. Vocation was a God-given call, or a younger son's right to hold a living 'owned' by the family. Like all stereotypes, there is some truth in this picture. Certainly old villagers in Suffolk remember when there was a parson for one village or two, and they were called 'Sir'. While there is often a desire for a recognizable local minister, a parson, there is also a need to watch the tendency to leave ministry to them. What does this suggest about encouraging rural ministerial vocation now?

This question led me to look at who the candidates for ministry in the church were. A rather superficial survey early in 2008 of 65 candidates and ordinands, and 15 people licensed in recent years as readers in the Diocese of St Edmundsbury and Ipswich, led to some interesting conclusions. The 80 people were from:

- towns (10,000 people or more and three-plus parishes);
- market towns (up to 10,000 population and one or two parishes);
- rural multi-parish benefices (over 50% of the population of St Edmundsbury and Ipswich diocese).

While this is not comprehensive, there were some broad conclusions that seemed to emerge from this sample:

1 From what I know of the candidates, the large majority are over 40 with only three in their twenties. There were slightly more women than men in the sample, and the genders are fairly evenly spread out over location and type of ministry.
2 In total, 80% of candidates for stipendiary ministry come from towns (55%) or market towns (25%).
3 About 70% of candidates for self-supporting ordained ministry come from the rural areas or market towns. Nearly half were from the rural multi-parish benefices. This figure rises to nearly 80% for reader candidates, with nearly 60% from rural areas.

4 The figures for self-supporting ordained ministry include the ordained local ministers (OLMs) trained on the Diocesan Ministry Course. Within the diocese as at 31 January 2008, there were 56 licensed OLMs compared to 13 deployable self-supporting ordained ministers (NSMs).

5 Interestingly, there were more born and bred Suffolk people exploring or entering ministry from the towns than the rural multi-parish benefices, where between 70% and 100% of all candidates for ordained ministers and readers are people who have moved into the area.

Such a small sample needs to be treated with caution, but is indicative of the present situation in the Diocese of St Edmundsbury and Ipswich. Since more vocations arise from towns, the figures suggest the relative difficulty of encouraging vocation to authorized ministry in rural areas. Perhaps this reflects little more than the population sizes. However, candidates for stipendiary ministry certainly seem to emerge from larger town churches and often, from my work with stipendiary curates, wish to return to similar situations for a curacy and first incumbency. Does this mean that rural incumbency is unattractive? While many find it challenging, many also perceive new opportunities and demands to articulate and live out the calling of the whole church. This cannot be achieved by solo ministry patterns. Once realized, this can release the incumbent's ministry as well as the ministry of others.

It is also interesting that a higher proportion of self-supporting ministers, both ordained and readers, are from rural parishes and this may be linked to the growing sense of need produced by pastoral reorganization. This links with a vocational theology that stresses ministry belongs to the whole church, but may also reflect that church-goers perceive the incumbent's need for help. Pragmatic need, a growing sense of the possibility of vocation to authorized ministry, and a desire to see the church broadening its impact on the community all form a strong rural pathway. The richer vocational theology of the church already expressed would help people engage with an understanding of God's activity that invites more than just a pragmatic approach to ministry.

Finally, looking at the statistics it is clear that long-term residents from rural multi-parish benefices are not well represented even in ordained local ministry (OLM), where they might be expected to feature prominently. Positively it should be noted that the rural church reflects the mixed populations of rural Suffolk – indeed, the sociological profile of OLMs in the diocese is very mixed. This suggests rural church communities are willing to form around the people who offer themselves and are duly trained for ministerial roles. But the question remains: why do so few original villagers offer themselves? While some do, others might be put off by prolonged selection and training. Others may feel, as suggested before, that to take a formal representative role is to push oneself forward in a way that others reject. One study indicates that villagers naturally have an association with the church that differs from the incomers' patterns of faith and commitment, which better suit the selection and training expectations.[12] Countering this may be a question of encouragement and support to build up involvement and confidence. One way this has been done is by encouraging groups from a single place to consider mission, vocation and ministry together:

Cathy, an OLM of some years' standing, originally explored her benefice's mission and ministry with a group of other people from the benefice, some of whom had a sense of vocation to authorized ministry. Although she herself did not, the group had a sense that she was being called to priesthood, which she fought and resisted all the way to a selection conference – and she still expresses surprise ten years on. She relates vocational language to her ordained ministry more than to her work as secretary within the local school. The latter provides a wide network of relationships, which means her ministry is called upon. She realizes and expresses that in some ways she has become vicar to her village and the stipendiary priest encourages this. The other members of the ministry team (another OLM and a reader) also tend to look after specific areas within the benefice.

This corporate and local discernment of vocation is very powerful and, with a training that emphasizes collaborative ministry, can build up a team of lay and ordained ministers who work together. This prevents Cathy's vocation being shaped by the older expectations that, as an ordained person, she does the ministry for the church. It is not about 'me and my ministry' but 'ours', a reflection of the corporate nature of a team approach. From observations here and in other provinces, it is easy for local shared ministry to slide back into old patterns, and a conscious effort to enable and facilitate others to consider their gifts and explore ministry and mission in their own settings is necessary.

Part of this is not to allow life to be too churchy. Cathy's work in the local school keeps her knowledge of the local villages broad and connected to what is happening beyond the confines of the church. The criteria for selection for ordained ministry and reader both recognize that vocation is a call to be realized not only in the church community, but in the communities beyond it as well. In theory, this should help prevent a fixation on simply keeping the rural multi-parish benefice running and focus the church on mission to the wider world, where there are so many rich opportunities.

Janice is retired and a reader within a busy rural multi-parish benefice; she says of her ministry:

More recently in Suffolk ministry has been more difficult than being overseas. For me, action has meant preaching as a reader in my parish and leading worship . . . This is the way I express my faith and my beliefs and try to lead others to faith. It now also means membership of the World Mission Group in the diocese. People find it very difficult to imagine the conditions in developing countries, but with my experiences . . . I can give a picture.

I responded to an invitation to become involved with the

local prison, first visiting as part of a group, then I led a Restorative Justice Programme. This six-week victim awareness course provides an opportunity for prisoners to reflect on the effect their crime has on other people.

There is always a need for Christian witness and action. And we all find the particular path which is for us.[13]

Janice had been a reader for some time, but this was not the end of her vocational pathway. Using her experience and commitment to the church overseas, and challenging her with a new task, has opened up her mission and ministry as a reader. Through her gifts and experiences she has broadened the horizon of her own vocation and that of the church. Too often, vocational language suggests a one-off event, a specific call to ministry of one type. But such a limited view ignores the God whose call reflects his ongoing actions as creator, redeemer and inspirer in individual lives and that of the church.

Both Cathy's and Janice's stories also reflect the second telltale sign of the whole church responding in mission and ministry. Working with other ministers to keep worship, mission and ministry alive and in encouraging others to be involved, they demonstrate an essential collaboration. Their experiences and vision broaden the understanding of what the church as a whole is called to respond to. They show the gospel reaching into many and various parts of life.

What do stories of incumbents suggest about their vocational pathway into rural ministry?

Stephen has moved from mostly suburban ministry to be incumbent of eight rural parishes. He had enjoyed some rural experiences through a college placement and part of his curacy. Moving from single parishes, he is struck by people's willingness to be involved to keep their church going, some even working to an idea of responsibility for the whole benefice. He enjoys working across the difference and variety in the churches and communities, the different ways of doing things, and the diverse social backgrounds of the people.

Rural ministry calls for a greater adaptability. As he gets used to it, he finds that some of the smaller management tasks are done by the individual parishes, actually leaving him time for pastoral work and leading worship.

Fiona had expected to move from a curacy into a city centre church with community involvement, but felt prompted to reply to an advert asking, 'Do you enjoy wearing wellies and relating to communities?' She could answer yes to both bits! The role being to be 'there for us', 'help say things we couldn't' to be the 'face of the church'. Being priestly in rural areas means to work at the boundaries as well as the centre of the church. With multi-parish benefices it is no longer possible to chair everything, gifts in others have to be liberated. But there can be frustrations about there not being enough people or time to achieve everything that is possible.

If vocation is not the once-and-for-all call, then both Stephen and Fiona have experienced the ongoing call to respond to God by uprooting from the known to go and experience the new challenges of rural mission and ministry. The picture they portray is a considerable shift from old patterns of 'my ministry' in 'my parish'.

Rather, authorized ministry is there to develop faithful, resilient, outward-looking rural church communities. Leading this across several distinctive communities, falls to them as incumbents. The selection criteria and learning outcomes for training increasingly stress the quality of collaboration and mission leadership for those who wish to be stipendiary clergy.

However, not all is new! Pastoral relationships are perhaps even more important because the incumbent in rural areas is more likely to be personally known by many within a community; the liturgical role remains essential and the need for prayer in, for and with the community is paramount. The multiplicity of parishes challenges the old model of working, but the theology with which this chapter began presents dynamic possibilities for the future. Incumbents and authorized ministers are called to find a new way of working with each other and the whole church. Not only does this need to avoid solo ministry, it also needs to shun possible new dangers that can either turn incumbents into chaplains of congregations denying their own role to be involved in mission in the wider community, or turn ministry teams into an oligarchy of authorized ministers.

Their task is to reflect on and bring into being the deeper call and gifting of the Spirit to the whole church. The report *Eucharistic Presidency* includes a phrase that says that the call of the ordained is: 'to promote, release and clarify all other ministries in such a way that they can exemplify and sustain . . . [the church's] oneness, holiness, catholicity and apostolicity'.[14]

The verbs 'promote', 'release' and 'clarify' are a more accurate approach to vocation of the ordained or authorized ministers within the gifted and called rural church of this moment.

Given the challenges and opportunities, how can we move forward?

Vocations, pathways and issues

- There is a need to communicate that a vocation to rural ministry is primarily about exploring new ways of being church and doing mission.
- Vocational courses and processes need to be developed that will help churches explore biblical teaching with both individuals and groups, and that allow a discernment of gifts in relation to mission needs. Sometimes a diocesan group is sufficient for this but, as Cathy's story suggests, more local groups link the possibility of vocation with an immediate awareness of need.
- There needs to be a continuing exploration of what collaboration means and what helps and hinders it. This is a priority for ministerial formation and training. The opportunity for stipendiary curates to work in rural benefices with self-supporting ministries of all kinds would help understanding and keep the mission focus broad.
- Pastoral reorganization should challenge clergy deanery

chapters to consider what consultancy, training and support would help them, other ministers and their churches engage theologically, spiritually and practically with change.

- A spiritual and training resource that equips teams alongside the leadership training provided for incumbents would help the outworking of the vocational theology contained here. Leadership initiatives need to resource people in the promoting, releasing and clarifying roles that will build up the sense of giftedness and the call to mission and ministry in individuals and the church.

- Tensions between what authorized ministers felt called to and what is being asked of them now need to be taken seriously in review systems. A ministerial development review needs to become an expectation for all ministers, in addition to continuing ministerial education. Where stress is acutely experienced, the Society of Martha and Mary, the Anglican Association of Advisers in Pastoral Care and Counselling,[15] and others can be turned to.

- Those applying ministerial discernment criteria need to be aware of rural ways of mission, where minister and congregation may be in many differing relationships with people. This too might be an issue in the selection of ministers where rural patterns of association may make mission different to suburban or urban models.

- More work needs to be done on why local rural people are reluctant to engage in authorized and representative ministry.

- Recent national reviews of training hoped for a greater resourcing of the whole church. Yet finances and the church's structures looked to the financing of the ordained first, other ministers second, and were not able to find national resources for education for discipleship. Is the effectiveness of trickle-down training through ministers to the local churches comparable to the effectiveness of trickle-down economics in changing the lot of the poor? Perhaps the challenge needs to go to dioceses and regional training partnerships to look at how training is done in order that it can work to the potential benefit of the whole church, as well as through ministers. This is especially true for rural areas where stipendiary resources are spread increasingly thinly across several communities. This would broaden vocational exploration and theological resources for the whole church.

A shared understanding of what it is God is calling the church and individuals to can help people re-engage with God's mission, and this is a dream not confined to just rural churches or this country. As one person has put it:

> Let us dream of a church with a radically renewed concept and practice of ministry . . . Where there is no clerical status and no classes of Christians, but all together know themselves to be part of the holy people of God. A ministering community rather than a community gathered around a minister.[16]

Questions

1 Given the development of the understanding of vocation, what do you see as the main roles of the ordained minister?

2 How can we encourage vocational questions based on the mission of the church rather than the need to keep the show on the road?

3 What does it mean to you to speak of the vocation of the whole church rather than speaking about people who have a vocation?

Notes

1 Tim Dearbon, *Beyond Duty: A Passion for Christ, a Heart for Mission*, MARC, 1998, quoted in *Mission-shaped Church*, London: Church House Publishing, 2002, p. 85.

2 The Central Board of Finance of the Church of England, *Eucharistic Presidency*, London: Church House Publishing, 1997, p. 20.

3 See Romans 12; 1 Corinthians 12; Ephesians 4.

4 1 Peter 1.1.

5 1 Peter 3.

6 World Council of Churches, *Baptism, Eucharist and Ministry*, Faith and Order Paper No. 111, Geneva: WCC, 1982, p. 17.

7 Stewart C. Zabrieskie, *Total Ministry: Reclaiming the Ministry of All God's People*, New York: The Alban Institute, 1995, p. 9.

8 General Synod Board of Education, *All Are Called – Towards a Theology of the Laity*, London: Church House Publishing, 1985, p. 4.

9 'Your Shape for God's Service'. Materials for six sessions for church groups, to help people discern their gifts for God's service. It is designed to be appropriate for all kinds of churches, including small ones. The materials are offered in a simple and flexible form so that they can be tailored and adapted to suit the context. There are no copyright restrictions. For more information, see http://www.carlislediocese.org.uk/ministry-and-vocation/everyday-life/Shape.html (accessed 3 March 2009).

10 For the Five Marks of Mission, see http://www.cofe.anglican.org/faith/mission/missionevangelism.html (accessed 3 March 2009).

11 Resources to carry out a simple parish audit are available from the Arthur Rank Centre, the churches' rural resources centre, see http://www.arthurrankcentre.org.uk.

12 Timothy Jenkins, *Religion in English Everyday Life – An Ethnographic Approach*, Oxford: Berghahn Books, 1999, pp. 43ff.

13 Diocese of St Edmundsbury and Ipswich DBF, *In Our Own Words: Readers' Experiences in the Community*, 2007, p. 9. Available from the Diocese of St Edmundsbury and Ipswich, Warden of Readers, c/o Diocesan Office, St Nicholas Centre, 4 Cutler Street, Ipswich, IP1 1UQ.

14 The Central Board of Finance of the Church of England, *Eucharistic Presidency*, p. 30.

15 For more information on the Anglican Association of Advisers in Pastoral Care and Counselling, see http://www.aaapcc.org.uk

16 Wesley Frensdorff, *The Dream: A Church Renewed*, Cincinnati: Forward Movement Publications, 1995, p. 8.

6

Lay leadership and lay development

ANNE RICHARDS AND JOANNA COX

Quite a rural part of the world, . . . West Country, lot of countryside folk there.

Bill Bailey, *Bewilderness*[1]

One of the challenges in looking at lay leadership and lay development in rural contexts is the way in which the church uses the word 'lay'. The language we use in describing the people of God in Christian congregations sometimes suggests that there can be a distinction between clergy and lay people in often monolithic terms. This can lead to presuppositions and assumptions not only about who clergy and lay people *are*, but also about the roles and functions of clergy and laity and what each can and cannot *do*. In some places, lay people in accredited lay ministry roles may not be recognized by the whole community, and they may feel they end up in a kind of no-man's-land between authorized minister and person in the pew. In other cases, there may even be stagnation and lethargy in which the people of God in a particular place are marking time waiting for something to happen. However, the argument of this chapter is that there are perspectives on lay leadership and development that show how much energy and potential is really there, and that it can be *especially* in rural contexts where it is found.

Here, four different methods are explored in which lay people and their contributions are particularly important in rural life and ministry. These are:

1 Lay presence and the theological significance of being lay.
2 The contribution of lay people to rural mission.
3 The particular importance of the gifting of lay people in rural leadership and development.
4 The role of rural lay people as having a prophetic visionary ministry to the whole church and to the wider world.

Each of the four sections starts with a short story illustrating the Christian lives of lay people in their particular communities. Theological themes are drawn out, before exploring what the story teaches about aspects of rural church life and practice. Some of the challenges and difficulties in getting things right are recognized, and some illustrative examples of positive developments in rural settings are included. The discussions are concluded in the last two sections by looking at a short case study, and briefly raising some ongoing issues that may be important to the future of the rural church.

Lay presence and the theological significance of being lay

The late Hilary Ineson sometimes used to comment, on emerging from some Church House meeting or other, that she felt especially 'lay' during the meeting. She did not mean that she felt excluded by the language or behaviour of the clergy at such times (although that could happen), but that she was aware, in her role as lay discipleship officer for the Church of England's National Board of Education, that she had a different perspective, experience and vision. This equipped her to view, and sometimes cut through, a mode of thinking about leadership and development that builds up in invisible layers, frustrating clergy, and led her to see being a lay Christian in terms of joy and freedom within vocation.

Implications

Rural ministry is sometimes felt to be an impossible task because there are too many churches and not enough clergy to go round, but less frequently acknowledged are ways in which the rural church often leads the way in teaching the wider church something about the whole community of God in ministry together. In fact, the rural church often allows lay people to model more directly Christian discipleship as revealed in scripture.

What is discipleship anyway? If we go to the New Testament, we can see that it involves vocation, obedience, service, community and journey. Jesus responded in obedience to the Father and called others to be with him. The disciples looked to Jesus as their teacher and guide, but were continually enjoined by him to realize that they could not take him for granted and to prepare for the time when they would be without his physical presence among them.[2] The disciples had to understand that they could not depend on Jesus to sort everything out (like the storm), but had themselves to form a fundamental relationship as human beings with God, and realize the place of faith in human flourishing. Their vocation, witness, acts of service and healing depended on receiving the wisdom and discernment to do God's will appropriately, rather than assuming that everything would just work. A lot of the time they had to learn this the hard way.

Jesus also insisted that their community was not based on a hierarchy of ability, holiness or some sort of spiritual merit, but on a gracious submission in service to one another and to God's people. The disciples did not lose their skills and jobs – indeed, they are seen fishing again before they encounter the resurrected Jesus in John 21. They were to function as a variously gifted but mutually enabling community. They made mistakes and learned lessons from these, and that too was part of discipleship. They did not usurp the role of Jesus after his death and resurrection, but lived in the Spirit such that Jesus was with them. The disciples therefore had to learn to live without the physical presence of Jesus, to work in ways that were always referential of Christ and to carry out ministry in Christ's name, not their own. This is discussed in detail in New Testament letters and illustrated through the Book of Acts. When faith failed them, ministry was ineffective. As friends and disciples, they worked out their spiritual journey together, sowing the seeds of new communities and laying the foundations for the future of the church.

Such discipleship can be seen in many rural areas, with lay people living as Christians and Christ continually being shown to others through them. This is indeed the primary ministry of all God's people. By contrast, the expectations of people outside the church are often that the only person with any proper authority in spiritual matters is the parish priest. This may have been reinforced through experience of the occasional offices, if those people have met only clergy in the process of interview, preparation and sacrament. What those same people often do not experience is the involvement of the whole discipled community.

The extent to which this way of being church is successful depends first on a proper understanding of the work of the Spirit in the communities being served, sustained and evangelized. It matters that lay people are seen as full participant members of the body of Christ, called and equipped by God to do his will. At the same time, each local Christian community is part of the larger body of Christ, and there needs to be a relationship with rural clergy that keeps the wider perspective and priestly witness meaningful and alive, even when those clergy cannot be there. Second, there needs to be more understanding of lay ministry continually equipped by the Spirit, and that has real effects in the community. Third, there needs to be the scope for that joy and freedom to be Christian people described by Hilary Ineson in the story that started this section. Where this works in rural churches, others in the community – who may never darken a church doorway – are often in no doubt that they are witnessing God's kingdom among them, with the local church being its cherished focus on which they depend for their own well-being.

Challenges

The church as a whole does not always engage with this model of ministry and discipleship, partly because it comes with challenges. Ministry and leadership, however you define them, however you train and equip for them, come shot through with complex issues about power and control. It is critical that these issues are not ignored in the process of training because misuse of power can be extremely difficult for a congregation and its community. This is true whether it is a matter of clergy refusing to collaborate effectively with laity, or lay people digging in against the clergy or, indeed, against each other.[3] Anglican church structures are, after all, traditionally hierarchical, organized around authority, bound by legal requirements, things you can and cannot do both to, and within, your rural church. With leadership and ministry comes serious and sometimes crippling responsibility. There is a continuous tension within the church about equipping, releasing, enabling, permission-giving and demonstrating, rather than just speaking of the freedom Christ offers.

Lay people may need training so as not merely to collude with clergy, particularly when clergy sometimes resort to direct delegation or apprenticeship models ('I'll show you and you do what I do') rather than collaborative ones ('We'll work on this together'). When the report on collaborative ministry, *A Time for Sharing*,[4] was being written, some interesting stories were collected. Some clergy felt disempowered, marginalized, or even questioned their vocations in the face of excellent lay leadership. Sometimes this provoked a backlash, with a desire to wrest back control, have the last word, or to curtail lay leadership that was getting away from the clergy. However, in other stories the presence of sensitively developed lay leadership was a source of relief, recuperation, encouragement, and friendship to clergy. It was very noticeable that these positive stories often came from rural situations, and were born not of trendiness or even theological conviction, but of a *necessity* for collaborative ministry.

Developments in practice

In one Oxfordshire village, it was decided to pay particular attention to Christian baptism as a starting point to affirm and encourage lay people as those called, discipled, entrusted and sent out into the world. In a tiny village, baptism was a fairly rare event, and an occasion significant enough to merit advertisement in the village newsletter to invite non-church-goers along. Also, whether the person baptized was an adult or a child, greater participation and interest from other members of that family often followed. The family of the baptized person was seen as a catechetical cluster, learning from and supporting one another. Through remembering baptism anniversaries and continued invitations, people were encouraged to see that baptism marks a decisive point in responding to God's call, so affirming and encouraging lay people to be partners and co-creators in God's calling. Building upon a sacrament that would take place anyway became particularly significant in affirming lay development. So, for example, the congregation celebrated 'a year in the life of' children who had been baptized the previous year and this generated prayer, pastoral care and recovery of people who found church a struggle.

One way in which Hereford diocese currently aims to develop local lay presence and the capacity of lay leadership is through offering developmental training for a variety of the traditional roles that need to be undertaken in the church and community. The programme rotates between sessions offered for churchwardens, treasurers, and PCC secretaries, held in various locations across the diocese. The training is designed to enable laity to develop confidence in their role and function as focal representatives of the church in small rural communities and as lay leaders. Sessions include discussion of case studies rooted in situations that could emerge locally.

The contribution of lay people to rural mission

A child who came to a harvest festival in a rural church was intrigued by some green things in a basket. They were pea pods, and the person who brought them into the church showed her how to shell the peas. The child was amazed and asked, 'How did you know they were there?' The gardener then told the child that there were many hidden treasures provided by God in nature: potatoes and carrots live under-ground, peas and nuts are contained in pods and shells. The gardener pointed out that animals know where to find God's hidden treasures, and thought it sad that many people don't know the same things. The child thought about it and said that people could recognize the beauty inside other people as God does, and it was also sad if that got missed or over-looked. This profound theological understanding came from specifically rural insights.

Implications

Lesslie Newbigin argued that the congregation is the herme-neutic of the gospel.[5] This has often been discussed in terms of urban models of being church, but it is perhaps especially true of the missionary potential of rural churches through the wit-ness of its laity to others. The extended worshipping community works towards being a model of kingdom and has an eschato-logical basis. This is not something that is dictated by the num-bers game; the hermeneutic of the gospel is as clear through the two or three gathered together as through a cast of thousands. What is particular about the lay contribution to this mission-ary understanding is the inclusiveness and ecumenical hospital-ity found in many rural churches. Rural congregations often exhibit the ability to exist in solidarity with those who suffer in the community, and to celebrate with and among the commu-nity. They may worship faithfully in ways that bring confidence, calm and hope to people who rarely attend church, but whose latent religious faith is nurtured by the few who are there.

It is important to ensure that training with congregations and clergy is not, consciously or unconsciously, based only on different models of congregation born out of suburban or urban experience. Development and training of lay people needs to affirm that even a couple of people in church on Sunday or at other services can be the foundational spiritual heart of a village community, on which the non-church-goers depend. Because of them, people come at Christmas, Harvest and Easter, and come for baptism, weddings and funerals. Church members need to encounter others and make connections that cannot be made any other way, by being aware of, and even mapping, where people *do* go. One matter that is often overlooked is the importance of elderly retired people in this walking of the gospel into people's lives. So it is not necessarily what jobs people have, but who they are that makes the significant difference. Often this takes place through the tourism industry[6] or centres around village shops and post offices, or networks in the village that depend on lay connections. It has been observed that activities such as dog walking in the countryside sets up the possibility for meeting, making friends and sharing thoughts and ideas in a non-threatening and unforced environment. This can allow people the opportunity to share something of their faith, belief and practice with others, as well as the opportunity to express pastoral concern, but those who are reluctant or lacking in confidence may need help to do this.

A study of one village[7] noted a series of important rituals – including meeting for beer and for sherry; crafts; shared and inclusive social events; tennis, croquet and bowls; doing flowers together and gardening – through which lay people met, shared and talked quite naturally about their faith as a matter of course. Each of these gathering activities took on a new force and focus when two young people from the village got married, both with learning difficulties and without any significant income. The preparation of the wedding dress, the flowers, reception and entertainment were shared village activities. More sherry was drunk than ever before! However, the event was not a matter of doing 'to' the couple. They were at the centre of the whole process, entirely loved and honoured by the community, and they brought an invigoration to the whole village, centred on their special day.

This means that encouraging and affirming the three 80-year-olds who make their way to church on Sunday is a legitimate means of expressing the hermeneutic of the gospel in that place. Cleaning churches and keeping them open, or nurturing wildflowers in the graveyard, have more missional impact than many realize. The rural church often has more opportunity to use its laity to keep alive a variety of church traditions and events that other parts of the church may see as backward or unfashionable, less entertaining, or just homogenized out of existence. These may include, for example, the vocational power of bells and music, and the language of the Book of Common Prayer. There is evidence from cathedrals and elsewhere that quiet services, especially early morning prayer, Eucharist and Compline are becoming more, not less, popular, as busy people search for peace. Visitors' books in the countryside often speak of the pleasure of peacefulness, a need to find rest and spiritual refreshment within the haven of a quiet open church. Yet this does not mean that the church has to be *empty* to give people what they are looking for. A quiet church with people at prayer, caring for the church or churchyard or simply offering quiet welcome can add a great deal to the tourist's experience of church as a lived-in and loved place of God.

Sensitive lay development can in consequence sometimes seem to fly in the face of the latest mission thinking. We can see this from the fact that good mission stories from rural churches do not always include Fresh Expressions, but have many kinds of less obvious outreach. Encouragement of lay people includes a need to allow lay people to *celebrate* their faith. This includes allowing people to love their church building, seeing that maintenance *can* be mission, and that one of the major contributions of the rural church to social capital is nothing less than an extension of that love to pride in village life and community.

Challenges

The difficulty with developing lay people to express ever more clearly the hermeneutic of the gospel as it is lived out in daily life is the danger of overburdening and burnout. Sensitivity has to be encouraged and the wisdom of discernment, so that jumping on new people who seem willing is resisted. Other challenges that present and that require management include the resenting of new ideas and problems of integration of incomers or 'townies'. Further challenges involve difficulties in persuading laity that they can be involved in priestly tasks rather than just assume the priest should do it. A particular tension can be about the use of extended communion or the virtue of a Service of the Word because there is little clarity about what it means to be a eucharistic community led by lay people. A number of these difficulties are illustrated in *The Grass Is Always Greener: Rural Life and Christian Faith*.[8]

Developments in practice

In a small group of rural parishes in Oxfordshire, a licensed lay reader paid a great deal of attention to local issues and interests and used them to inform whatever she did in church. Intercessions and thanksgiving were generated by local events and remembered occasions, and then linked to the needs of the wider world. People were invited to tell stories and give short presentations as part of the congregational prayers. The reader also used local issues interwoven with scripture in preaching and encouraged local people both inside and outside the church to see themselves as people of the parables: 'When Hugh went out to sow his fields last week, he noticed that some of the seed fell on to the stony track at the edge of Field Lane . . .' She also did a great deal to make people from other Christian denominations feel welcome in the churches, asking them what their favourite hymns were, and suggesting that they be included in worship. Church attendance grew in several of the parishes, clergy responded by nurturing the newcomers and developing further lay people's gifts for welcome, visiting and hospitality. This meant that when clergy moved on there was an underlying network of pastoral care and worship practice that helped to keep the congregations together during vacancies.

In a rural parish in Gloucestershire, it was realized that the creation of a multi-parish benefice changed the pattern of liaison between a parish church and its local church primary school. A group of parishioners formed a team to take responsibility for the link between church and school. As a group, they also took turns with clergy on the rota for leading collective worship in the school.

A diocesan officer working with rural parishes encourages lay people to think about aspects of their mission. Using the metaphor of the compass to look towards reframing the life and ministry of the rural church today, this stresses the importance of looking at different directions where mission can occur. The material examines changes in rural living as it affects lay people, energizes them for the potential and opportunities of rural Christian living and, most interestingly, sets the active life of lay Christians in rural situations within the wider context of the greater church. The potential energy of the rural church is seen as a contribution to equipping the church at large in an outward-looking, mission-oriented perspective that is carried and nurtured by lay people. The programme looks firmly at a future of growth and spiritual depth, powered and enabled by lay people.[9]

Potential gifts in the whole body

Joanna writes: 'Remote in the African bush, I went to small traditional villages, where a priest visited only once a month. The Christian communities were nevertheless thriving: organizing prayer groups, women's sewing clubs, confirmation classes and retreat days. When I first arrived as a teacher from London I was surprised by this, wondering how these tasks could be undertaken so successfully by people with no formal theological college (or indeed post-primary school) training. As I stayed longer, the question changed. Why weren't lay people in England taking on such initiatives and responsibilities? And I also then realized that I was only surprised because I had never previously stopped to question my presuppositions about how the church could be organized, or my assumptions that certain tasks would be undertaken by clergy.'

Implications

It is a fundamental theological concept that all human beings are called by God to partnership in his reconciling, restorative work at the heart of creation. J. V. Taylor tells us clearly about this universality in his set of Bible studies called *The Uncancelled Mandate*.[10] This insight lay at the heart of the key report entitled *All Are Called*.[11] What this means is that every human being is potentially tasked and gifted for a particular contribution to the body of Christ, even though not all accept the call. For some, the calling is to carry out tasks in the community and outside the church; others experience a call to faithful service within a congregation. Some respond to a call to ordination, often nurtured and encouraged by the lay community from which they come. Lay development and training in rural contexts requires a careful understanding of the importance of all forms of vocation, what particular callings require, how they are expressed in the church and community, what their tremendous potential entails, and what God intends through them.

The iconic importance of the church building in many rural villages can sometimes result in the church being seen only in terms of place, with the contribution of lay Christians being thought of as secondary. During worship the congregation proclaims 'we are the body of Christ'. But people's actions do not always fully reflect the implications of the Pauline metaphor, or witness to the potential of a church made up of different members with different gifts. The metaphor recognizes a God-given giftedness of each individual.

Church culture has often dominated theological insights, recognizing the importance of the contributions of the whole people of God to building up the body. Ministry, like mission, has in the past frequently been seen as the preserve of the clergy. Yet reflecting on church leadership and ministry in a biblical perspective, Paul Stevens writes: 'Rather than having the church assist them to do the work of ministry, leaders are assistants to the rest of the body to empower them for their service in church and world.'[12]

Rural communities can be places where the very varied gifts of individuals are recognized. The complex web of established relationships in some rural areas may result in a particular need for individuals to be invited, and given permission to use their gifts when they would not otherwise do so. It is essential that clergy recognize the significance of their role in this regard. The church can then become a place to celebrate and affirm these gifts, and the ministry and discipleship offered both within the church and in the wider world.

There may be a range of reasons why this does not always happen and why low-key contributions may not be celebrated by the church. There can be fears that the focus on giftedness may mean that people will become valued for what they do rather than unconditionally accepted as children of God, and the spiritual heart of the church may get less attention.

Exploring the gifts God gives to each person can nevertheless be valuable.

- The concept of gift can help acknowledge difference without it being based on social status or tradition, so baptizing the concept of difference.
- It can recognize the interconnectedness of differing gifts, and so the need for all within the community to contribute something, whether large or small.
- It can affirm giftedness as God-given, not just a pragmatic convenience that will enable jobs to be done.
- It potentially enables the church to recognize, affirm and develop widely different contributions to church and com-

munity across an entire congregation – for example, the value of Christian hospitality or links with schools.

- Looking at giftedness can affirm the value of all people and avoid hierarchical understandings of 'first-rate' or 'second-rate' ministry. This can also be valuable in situations where there are very differing approaches to ministry from those new to the rural community, who may be more willing to take on formal or accredited roles such as reader.
- Recognizing the gifts that are present in a congregation may be an important tool in discerning its corporate vocation.

Across the Anglican Communion, rural situations have spawned some of the most imaginative pioneering experiments in developing and supporting lay ministry. In North America, the Dioceses of Northern Michigan and Nevada have been forerunners, followed by other Anglican dioceses in Canada, New Zealand and within the Episcopal Church in the USA. These developments have been given a variety of names, including 'Mutual Ministry' and 'Total Ministry', and described as 'an approach to Christian ministry that is lived out of the promises made in baptism. It sees the ministry of the whole congregation as the primary ministry.'[13]

Challenges

One legacy of Christendom is that the church is deeply embedded in the social context. As a consequence, it can become increasingly hard to distinguish different aspects of the church. The building, the organizational church structures, the regular events, spiritual truths and the Christian community can all sometimes be seen as the church 'as it was in the beginning, is now, and shall be for ever'. There can be deeply differing approaches to church from long-term residents and new arrivals. For those with established roots in an area, the church can be an essential element in a sense of identity, with ancestors in the graveyard, for example. On the other hand, newcomers may bring different assumptions about church from elsewhere.

They often expect the church to be visibly alive and pro-active, and may be more driven and impatient with what they see as resistance to change.

Developments in practice

Some dioceses currently plan and offer training to encourage and affirm this understanding of God-given giftings. Carlisle diocese has developed a short six-session course called *Your Shape for God's Service*.[14] This is particularly appropriate in rural areas: it grew out of a recognition that much existing published material looking at giftedness presupposed much larger gathered congregations. This course was designed and extensively piloted in rural congregations, with exercises and activities that are non-threatening and suitable for small groups. It has also been designed so that it can be adapted for use in other dioceses where appropriate and positive reports have likewise been returned from other users.

The Scottish Episcopal Church has many far-flung rural congregations. They have developed a pattern of working alongside the whole of the congregation, rather than just some individuals within it. This supports what they describe as local collaborative ministry (LCM), with the idea of baptismal ministry at its heart. When a congregation is exploring the possibility of formally becoming a LCM congregation, they are asked to look at the implications of baptismal calling both individually and corporately. Each person is asked, 'How are you called to live out your baptism in your individual life context: at home, work, recreation?' The congregation as a whole is asked, 'How are you called to be the church in this local context?' and to produce a mission plan. The experience of some congregations has been a positive and affirming one. As one who has experienced this writes:

On the journey to becoming self-sustaining, relationships alter dramatically from being those of competition and threat to those of support and encouragement. This is seen most clearly in terms of the diocese where personal Episcopal oversight is enjoyed rather than being perceived as control. LCM congregations value their Bishops because they know they really need them – not just to do the special liturgical rites – but as part and parcel of their collaborative life, as friends, guides and mentors.[15]

The role of rural lay people in visionary ministry

An American couple came to Britain for an Air Force event remembering the veterans of World War II. While they were in Britain, they went to church in the local village where the veteran believed he had once had relatives. Looking through the records did not reveal anything very significant. As they walked among the gravestones, an elderly villager passing by engaged them in conversation and recognized the name. In the course of discussing his memories of people related to the family, he remembered a particular feud over the owner-ship of a field. Intrigued, the American couple went to visit the remnants of the other family, only to discover that the grudges and memories were still fresh. After talking about the rights and wrongs of the past feud and through making friends and exchanging gifts, the rift was healed. The Ameri-can couple went home feeling they had discovered important roots. The other family started coming back to church.

Implications

The term 'prophecy' can be understood by some to relate only to knowledge of the future and very specific events that will occur: the definition we use is deeper, wider and more vision-ary. Christian people are invested with prophetic insight and vision such that through faith they can provide a description not only of what is wrong with human life, but also a vision of how it might be both reconciled and restored.

Mission theology draws attention to the importance of vision and prophetic ministry. For example, a recent ecumenical publication, *Journey into Growth*,[16] describes the focusing of vision as 'a spiritual exercise of discerning how God wants to lead your Christian community. It's discovering and naming what makes your church heartbeat tick.'

Christian lay people need to be equipped and empowered to share that insight and work for restoration. Walter Wink has argued for a kind of spirituality audit that discerns the 'angel' of a church, in which the quality, gifting and potential of a congregation is assessed over time.[17] The importance of lay people to this process cannot be overestimated: it is the people who hold the memory of the church who are able to provide the longitudinal understanding of what a church has meant to a community, and what its story still provides to those living in the area. This kind of work, which is important to the mission of a congregation, cannot so easily be done by clergy without a significant time investment.

The significant prophetic role of lay people also extends to prayer and worship. Lay people are interactive between the experience of living alongside or within such events and bringing them into church for intercession. In events such as farming crises, closure of post offices, shops and schools, and people going to hospital, they can hold the problems and joys of a community in offering to God. The lay potential of intercession as prophetic lament and as a programme for pastoral action is often misunderstood and certainly underused. In rural areas, laity can also be instrumental in bringing insights about how cyclical events such as lambing and harvest mesh with the church's own cycles of learning and celebration.

In rural areas where particular families have existed for generations, some lay people may have insights into others' abilities and gifts, and be able to encourage their involvement in ways that incoming clergy cannot. Lay people may also be those who hold memory, tradition and faithfulness of the church. They often have the ability to focus, speak of and represent rural difficulty and rural possibility and need encouragement, and sometimes permission, to do so.

One way to do this is for the church community to develop

memory traditions, which look for and enable the telling of a faith story as life stories. For example, a retired country doctor who had looked after families in isolated rural areas during the war would often tell children about performing emergency baptisms of babies he thought would not live. His explanation of why he did this, rather than try medical heroics, profoundly affected the young people to whom he told these stories, giving faith action a credibility and importance that they had not previously thought about. In this way, deep latent religious feeling can be energized into commitment by lay people, often, as in this case, over many years.

Challenges

One principal difficulty in enabling lay ministry of this kind is a misunderstanding of what prophetic and visionary ministry in the countryside looks like. For example, lay people holding memory or the 'angel' of a church can be misunderstood as exhibiting stick-in-the-mud attitudes and resistance to change. This has been seen in refusals to re-order churches, dislike of Common Worship, resentment of incomers, and resistance to evangelistic initiatives. This points to a difficulty of recognizing a prophetic ministry and releasing the history and memory of a worshipping community to shape and form new congregational patterns and growth.

Developments in practice

A parish in Cornwall faced a vacancy and parishioners were aware that they would in future be linked with other parishes as part of the pastoral reorganization. A group of three lay people (one a churchwarden) were aware of the need for the church to develop new patterns, and the fact that they did not need to wait for a new incumbent to arrive before starting to look forward. As soon as the vacancy began, they contacted diocesan officers, and arranged for training and support in the parish. They recognized that as a multi-parish benefice it could be helpful to develop some non-eucharistic worship, and encouraged some people to participate in a group to share leading worship. They gave others in the congregation confidence to participate in a new parish pastoral care group. Their vision and prophetic ministry helped shape and prepare for a new and appropriate pattern of congregational ministry, which the future incumbent was able to develop.

A case study

A small north Buckinghamshire village is part of a multi-parish benefice with no resident clergy. For many years, the church building had been open only for services, but a lay member of the congregation felt convinced that the community would value the church being open and available to all outside times of worship. She raised the issue with the PCC. The response was that it would indeed be nice for the church to be open more, but the group immediately recollected past problems and raised a long list of practical difficulties and complications. In the face of this resistance, the determination and vision of a single lay person was the deciding factor. Against the odds, she worked out practical strategies and gathered a team to help, managing to solve practical problems without creating confrontation. She took on the ongoing responsibility of ensuring the church was locked and unlocked at weekends.

Encouraging the church to be opened was a local lay initiative. It demonstrated the value of lay Christian presence where missionary and prophetic vision are combined with gifts of organization and the ability to encourage and involve others. A lay woman's ministry offered the key, both literally and metaphorically, that enabled the church to be more open to the community.

Future issues

Lay leadership and development in rural areas needs to be understood, properly equipped and carefully encouraged. Rural churches have the opportunity to be frontrunners in providing models of how to be church in terms of discipleship, especially where there are more fluid boundaries between church and community, as research on the contribution of the rural church to social capital has shown.[18]

Small congregations are a facet of rural communities. All too often this is viewed with dismay, and seen as the proverbial glass as half full or, indeed, *less* than half full! But others have discovered that a positive result of tiny congregations is that they know they have to learn to co-operate and collaborate with others, rather than attempt to be closed self-sufficient communities. As a result, some of the most positive examples of collaborative ministry have emerged in rural areas.

Christian lay people in rural areas are gifts to their communities and to the church. However, alongside examples of creative initiatives, elsewhere many laity are not effective disciples because they feel undervalued, over-controlled or improperly used. Others have never been encouraged to move beyond a habit of dependency within the church community. Within small communities, often with a range of patterns and practices that have to some extent become hallowed by time, the tasks of encouraging and permission giving can be of enormous importance. Other lay people and clergy can have an important role here.

If there is to be effective lay development and leadership there has to be adequate training for all involved, and a recognition that ongoing support and encouragement are needed. Recent strategic thinking in mission and in prophetic ministry, such as local or collaborative ministry schemes, requires clergy and lay people together to be trained in matters such as double listening to the church and community. They need to grow in ongoing discernment of the needs of rural communities and understanding of the issues of sustainability. Any team serving multi-parish benefices needs to incorporate lay people, and resources made available to ensure their potentials can be maximized.

All lay people are 'the people of his pasture, and the sheep of his hand'.[19] If the sheep are to be fed, it is not just because they are hungry or cannot feed themselves. It is so that they may grow, graze land, provide sustenance, clothe others and to make more of themselves: the recognizable marks of their mission and presence in the countryside.

Questions

1 What are the main potentials for developing lay leadership in your own situation?

2 What are the main obstacles to further lay leadership and development in your own situation?

3 What range of different gifts can you distinguish among the clergy and laity in your situation and how could they be developed further for shared ministry?

Notes

1 Bill Bailey, *Bewilderness*, 2005, Universal Studios.

2 John 13.33, 36; compare John 7.33–36; 8.21.

3 This important issue is examined in more depth in *Presence and Prophecy: A Heart for Mission in Theological Education*, London: Church House Publishing, 2002, pp. 63–6.

4 *A Time for Sharing: Collaborative Ministry in Mission*, London: Board of Mission of the General Synod of the Church of England, 1995.

5 Lesslie Newbigin, *The Gospel in a Pluralist Society*, London: SPCK, 1989.

6 For example, one person who makes a living taking people on fishing trips finds such occasions of time and space a good opportunity to talk about his faith with others.

7 Undertaken by Anne Richards.

8 *The Grass Is Always Greener: Rural Life and Christian Faith*, London: Church House Publishing, 2002.

9 An initiative within the Diocese of Gloucester.

10 Board of Mission of the General Synod of the Church of England, *The Uncancelled Mandate*, London: Church House Publishing, 1998.

11 General Synod Board of Education, *All Are Called – Towards a Theology of the Laity*, London: Church House Publishing, 1985.

12 R. Paul Stevens, *The Abolition of the Laity*, Carlisle: Paternoster Press, 1999, p. 149.

13 *Mutual Ministry*, The Ministry Development Office of the Episcopal Church, http://www.episcopalchurch.org/19625_14838_ENG_HTM.htm (accessed 3 March 2009).

14 *Your Shape for God's Service*. Materials for six sessions for church groups, to help people discern their gifts for God's service. It is designed to be appropriate for all kinds of churches, including small ones. The materials are offered in a simple and flexible form so that they can be tailored and adapted to suit the context. There are no copyright restrictions. For more information, see http://www.carlislediocese.org.uk/ministry-and-vocation/everyday-life/Shape.html (accessed 3 March 2009).

15 Tim Morris, *Local Collaborative Ministry in the Scottish Episcopal Church*, 2007, p. 4, http://www.scotland.anglican.org/media/organisation/boards_committees/lcm/files/lcm_in_the_sec.pdf (accessed 3 March 2009).

16 Terry Tennens (ed.), *Journey into Growth*, London: Churches Together in Britain and Ireland, 2007, p. 14.

17 Walter Wink, *Unmasking the Powers*, Minneapolis: Fortress Press, 1986, pp. 73–86. The concept of a 'spirituality audit' for churches has also been developed by Robert Warren.

18 R. Farnell, J. Hopkinson, D. Jarvis, J. Martineau and J. Ricketts Hein, *Faith in Rural Communities: Contributions of Social Capital to Community Vibrancy*, Stoneleigh Park: Acora Publishing, 2006.

19 Psalm 95.7.

7

A vision for Initial Ministerial Education

MARTYN PERCY

Not so long ago, the village of Elmdon could justly claim to be one of the most studied rural communities in England. Two anthropologists, Marilyn Strathern[1] and Jean Robin,[2] published their ground-breaking studies that explored the changing face of village life in rural Essex, and how these communities were evolving. Robin's study charted continuity and change in village identity from the mid-nineteenth century through to the 1960s. Covering the ownership of land, labour, farming, marriage and social mobility, it is one of the first analyses that points to the present context of a typical rural village today: namely, profound shifts in the composition of such communities; yet at the same time a sense of continuity with the past that seems to be remarkably resilient.

Similarly, Strathern was able to map the underlying value-systems that seemed to shape community identity. This included the persistent notion of a 'Real Elmdon' (used to distinguish it from anything apparently alien or new), which she maintained was held through tightly formed patterns of kinship. Indeed, Strathern argued that the concept of kinship provided a vital key to understanding the delicate way in which the community was arranged. Kinship cuts across employment, class, gender and other apparent divisions, and identifies who 'really belongs' and who has yet to be integrated. To 'outsiders', the question as to who is a 'real' villager may seem unnecessarily parochial and quirky. Strathern showed, however, that kinship played a vital role in identifying Elmdon.

Both Robin and Strathern were able to foresee something of what the future might hold for villages such as Elmdon towards the end of the twentieth century and the beginning of the twenty-first. Factors included increasing numbers of commuters, who would slowly turn the community into a predominantly dormitory village. Less work would be available for local people, as rural industries changed or disappeared. Rising house prices would force some settled and established forms of kinship to become more attenuated, as the economic pressures caused greater degrees of familial dispersal. The effect of this, ironically, is often to intensify a sense of community identity. Resilience is manifested in both resistance and accommodation. Indeed, this kind of outlook can powerfully influence the whole approach to rural ministry, especially in the occasional offices.[3]

Yet despite the depth of their ethnography and anthropological analysis, Robin and Strathern devoted little time to the church itself. This omission is understandable, in some sense. The blindness to the presence of the church arises directly out of a collation of social sciences that colluded with the classic secularization theses from the 1960s. These tended to stress the increasing impotency of established religion, and assumed that its residual power lay merely in rituals that affirmed kinship, ties to the land, the capacity to engage folk religion, and the rites of passage that marked generational continuity and change. The authors therefore might be surprised to see that many rural churches are surviving in the twenty-first century, or even flourishing, occupying a pivotal position in their respective communities. In some cases, the church will be the sole public community building remaining; not only a spiritual amenity, but also a place for the whole village to gather. In other cases, the church will have a key role in supporting or hosting a post office or small shop, and acting as a conduit for a range of voluntary and care services.

As David Martin[4] has noted, churches are markers and

anchors in many rural communities; with the primary or sole repository of all-embracing meanings pointing beyond the immediate to the ultimate. Rural churches are institutions that deal in tears and concern themselves with the breaking points of human existence. They provide frames of reference, narratives and signs to live by. And they continue to offer persistent points of reference that are beyond consumerism, fashion or other forms of transitory existence. This is why burial places can be so important, the availability of a public space that still enables a real relationship between the living and the dead to be appropriately maintained. Moreover, this is not mere maintenance. Rather, it is mission, providing the space in which people can live and move and have their being, within a context of bereavement and its attendant ministry.

Contemporary English church-going habits correlate with the two main religious economies that can be observed in Europe. The first is a market model, which assumes voluntary membership will soon become the norm. The second model is utility, where membership is ascribed rather than chosen. In the first model, individuals opt in to become members. In the second model, all in some sense are deemed to belong, unless they opt out. The two models are in partial tension, and arguably depend upon each other. One may further characterize these differences as 'intensive' and 'extensive' forms of ecclesial polity. Some sociologists of religion think the extensive will not be able to survive without the intensive. Some ecclesiologists think that the intensive is fundamentally dependent upon the extensive.

The dominant paradigm for rural ministry in England is essentially 'utility-extensive'. Indeed, many forms of 'market-intensive' ecclesial polity have been evaporating from English villages in the post-war era, often leaving Anglican churches and ministers to cater for residual non-conformist congregations. Correspondingly, appropriate initial and continuing ministerial training may need to pay careful attention to a variety of relationships. These could include, for example, land and people; economy and ecosystems; tradition and values;

continuity and innovation; constructions of local identity; politics and culture; collaboration and rivalry. It must also work within contexts that are simultaneously delicate and robust, as well as reticulate, subtle and discrete.

The nature of contemporary rural life places some interesting demands and challenges upon the ministry of the church. These include the recognition that the somewhat dubious distinction between mission and maintenance, so easily assumed in urban and suburban contexts, is a false dichotomy in the majority of rural contexts. Good maintenance is likely to be, de facto, good mission. It involves and affirms the wider community, thereby nourishing social and spiritual capital. The relationship between a church and its people in many rural village contexts is essentially perichoretic: the 'mutual indwelling' of various cultural and religious currents that blend and inter-penetrate, yet also maintain their distinctive identities.

This is especially suggestive for ministerial formation and education. Quality may need to be valued more than quantity. Affirming the resonance of the past may have a higher spiritual value than the apparent obviousness of the need for relevance and progress. Presence and deep relational engagement may have a greater missiological impact than overt evangelistic schema and initiatives. The ministerial blend of being and doing (the clergyperson as both contemplative and activist) may need to be adjusted in any transition from urban or suburban contexts to rural ministry. Because rural ministry may only have one professional clergyperson for several parishes, she or he will normally fare better as a generalist than as a specialist; as a person of breadth and accommodation rather than being overly particular in theological outlook; of accepting the prioritization of extensity (partly brought about by there being less choice) instead of the comfort of distinctive intensity.

Lest this sound too romantic – and the reality of rural ministry is that it often suffers from being misconstrued as some kind of idyll-type activity – there can be no question that recent political, economic and cultural challenges have transformed the landscape of perception. While every generation that has ever lived has faced its own modernity, the rural ministry of today is clearly different to that which was known by George Herbert, Parson Woodforde and other classic exemplars from previous centuries. Rural ministry is now, arguably, at the cutting edge of the church (the most obvious and identifiable model of 'utility-extensive' ecclesial polity, and therefore of classic English Anglicanism); is therefore sustainable, as well as under threat; and is one of the more challenging and rewarding contexts for ministry at present.

But what kind of preparation is needed for this ministry? The first and most obvious thing to say about the purpose of ordination training, formation and education for ordained ministry is that it is not immediately obvious. What, after all, is one being prepared for? As Urban Holmes III presciently observed more than 30 years ago, the roles and tasks of the clergy were not nearly as palpable in the late twentieth century as they might have been 100 years earlier. It almost goes without saying that if the professional status of clergy is somewhat ambivalent, then the training and formation that seminarians (or ordinands) receive is also likely to reflect this.

Yet this is not quite so. Students preparing for ordained ministry, in whatever institution they are being trained, formed and educated, can point to a curriculum (usually with a multiplicity of options, but also a core); some kind of disciplined approach to prayer and worship; an ecclesial tradition that adds some kind of accent to the ethos of the institution; some practical assignments that continue to test the depth and trajectory of a vocation; and a continuous process of theological reflection that links the personal, social, intellectual and transcendent dynamics of formation. It is purposeful, too, as this rather light-hearted (but affectionate) description suggests:

> Our ordinands are only allowed to graze on the richest, most fertile theology. We don't use artificial preservatives, cut corners or mass-produce to grow our students. We simply combine centuries of tradition and know-how with wisdom and new insights. This natural diet is complemented by a

fresh, open, organic approach to formation which, together with our own cutting-edge research, provides them with some of the finest training pastures available.

We hope you like the results: super, natural clergy.[5]

Yet such a sketchy and skeletal outline of the priorities for theological education affords considerable licence to any ecclesial tradition and its training institutions. What, then, can be said about Anglican theological education? And what of formation and training for rural ministry?

Over the past three decades, the Church of England has witnessed a number of quite significant sea-changes in the profile and delivery of formation and training for ordained ministry. In the mid-1970s, almost three-quarters of ordinands were under the age of 30. Today, that figure has dropped to a little over 10% of the total numbers in training, almost the same as those in training over the age of 60. The average age of ordination is now around 40. Correspondingly, there has been a significant shift in the expectations provided through training. Ordinands enter colleges and courses with significantly more life experience and maturity. They are also likely to be of similar age to the teaching staff, which has inevitably led to the development of more consensual and negotiated patterns of training, in place of programmes that might have once been simply imposed.

To complement this development, the Church of England has also witnessed a significant change in the range of contexts for formation and training. Thirty years ago, more than two-thirds of ordinands trained in residential colleges, with part-time training in non-residential courses a relative novelty. The tables are almost entirely turned at the beginning of the twenty-first century, with the majority of ordinands now being formed on a variety of non-residential courses. So although six of the eleven residential colleges are broadly evangelical (reflecting the popularity of that wing of the church), there are over a dozen regional training schemes and ordained local ministry courses. The latter are ecclesiologically and theologically broad, continuing to reflect the historic strength of English spiritual proclivity for openness. This is an articulate, conversational and inclusive breadth that serves the whole needs of the rural parish, rather than the kind of particular confessional stance that might be afforded through the choices available within the fundamentally competitive and consumerist expressions that arise in suburban or urban contexts.

At the core of training and formation for ministry, and this will be true for almost all Anglican training institutions, is a commitment to interweaving theology with experience, and usually in some kind of dynamic reflective practice. Often this is done through the exercise of ministry: observing, participating, leading and then reflecting. In such a context, the experiences of ordinands can often be quite turbulent before they become fulfilling. They may undergo a process of 'dis-memberment' before 're-membering', as they encounter a range of experiences and practices that can comfort and disturb in equal measure. The teaching underpinning this activity will most likely be constructive. Yet the very act of education (from *educare* – to literally draw out) can be costly, but an essential prerequisite to the process of transformation that ministerial formation is concerned with, and perhaps especially in rural contexts. As James Hopewell perceptively observes:

> Rather than assume that the primary task of ministry is to alter the congregation, church leaders should make a prior commitment to understand the given nature of the object they propose to improve. Many strategies for operating upon local churches are uninformed about the cultural constitution of the parish; many schemes are themselves exponents of the culture they seek to overcome.[6]

One might add a loud 'Amen' to such sentiments. But what exactly does Hopewell mean when he suggests that clergy are often 'uninformed about the cultural constitution of the parish'? One fertile notion that comes from the vocabulary of sommeliers might be helpful here. *Terroir* is a Gallic word for which there is no English equivalent. The term refers to the combination of factors that make one wine slightly different from another, even when they are geographically proximate. Sunshine and temperature; north or south facing, and the amount of rainfall; the height of the land and the drainage; the type and acidity of the soil; the types and subtypes of grape, and their progeny; local know-how and human skill; the amount of time permitted for a wine to mature, and the types of barrels chosen – all combine to make wines taste different.

This accounts for why one Burgundy tastes quite different from another, even though they might be from the same village. And this analogy has something to teach theologians as they reflect on the composition of local ecclesial identity. On one level, church is church, just as wine is wine. Yet to the refined palate, the differences are detectable and telling. The ecclesial history and ethos of one rural church might be composed through all manner of stories, buildings, forms of organization, ecclesial and theological accents; and in an adjacent church, yet in a similar context, turn out to be entirely different. And, arguably, it is only through deep and patient immersion and reflection, the refining of the palate in effect, that good mission can be undertaken.

The ecclesial *terroir*, in other words, is something that a minister needs to be able to read sensitively and deeply if he or she is to cultivate congregational life and offer connected parochial ministry. Moreover, if a minister is overseeing several rural churches, their clustering together, for organizational purposes, will seldom disguise the fact that although roughly proximate, each congregation will have a slightly different feel, flavour, history and dialect. (Rather as in anthropological terms, as neighbouring tribes in a given place can be very different. Indeed, the surfacing and expression of difference is what makes identity possible.) So ministerial formation and training will, at this point, need to find ways of providing deeper forms of discernment that enable ministers to move beyond the surface or presenting task of demand-led organization, and make time and space to read each congregation and parish as a semi-discrete but related, locally distinctive expression of Christian faith.

These brief remarks are perhaps especially suggestive for rural ministry, but also for formation and theological education more generally, whether in residential or non-residential contexts. Context may indeed have a direct bearing on theological output. In other words, theology can be a rather slow discipline; it takes time to accrue wisdom for the journey. Part of the process of formation is to comprehend the vision for theological reflection, which is attending patiently and deliberately to all kinds of material. This means helping ordinands to 'loiter with intention' (or 'deep hanging out', as the anthropologist Clifford Geertz puts it) within issues and over encounters; to consciously and purposefully dawdle in their deliberations, so that clarity and wisdom comes to fruition. Theology is not a discipline for hurrying.

Arguably, Karl Barth understood something of the necessary patience required in rural ministry, and from his Swiss canton he penned these words:

> The true growth which is the secret of the upbuilding of the community is not extensive but intensive; its vertical growth in height and depth . . . It is not the case that its intensive increase necessarily involves an extensive. We cannot, therefore, strive for vertical renewal merely to produce greater horizontal extension and a wider audience . . . If it [the Church and its mission] is used only as a means of extensive renewal, the internal will at once lose its meaning and power. It can be fulfilled only for its own sake, and then – unplanned and unarranged – it will bear its own fruits.[7]

But what might Barth mean by this? He has several things in mind, but for the purposes of this chapter, three merit noting. First, that rural churches and ministries may need to be genuinely patient and resilient. They have vested interests in continuity and perpetuity. This means that a quick results-oriented immediacy often has to be set aside in favour of something more natural, organic and slower. Sustaining and maintaining is as important as changing. Second, there is a sense in which Barth clearly understands our earlier reference to utility-extensity and market-intensity models of the church. And theologically, Barth graciously points out that intensity cannot be adopted in order to produce extensity. Third, Barth goes some way to redeeming the notion of intensity, by suggesting that a more concentrated focus on God is at the heart of all good ministry, but that this does not necessarily lead to the kind of extensive growth one might witness in a city or suburban context. Quality of discipleship – in other words, the sheer faithfulness of ministries – may not necessarily lead to quantifiable results.

So what of a vision for formation and training for ministry in rural contexts? Jesus, interestingly, offers quite a range of powerful organic or natural metaphors that may be of some help to us here. But I want to focus on just two for the moment: yeast and salt. 'He told them another parable: "The kingdom of heaven is like yeast that a woman took and mixed in with three measures of flour until all of it was leavened.""[8]

Here, Jesus tells us most of what we probably need to know about ministry. He suggests that the kingdom of heaven is like yeast that is mixed in with dough. Yeast? That microbe fungi? That discardable and forgettable material that is, oddly, the key to so much of our lives? It would seem so. For yeast is what ferments the wine and beer; and it makes the dough rise to make the bread. It is the tiny, insignificant catalyst for our basic commodities and the formation of our communities. The leaven in the lump; the difference between bread and dough; juice and wine; refreshment and celebration.

Yeast is, of course, small. Moreover, it is lost and dispersed into the higher purposes to which it is given. And when Jesus talks about the kingdom of God as yeast, and our ministries too, he is not advocating the concentrate of Marmite in a jar: yeast for the sake of yeast. Rather, in Jesus' imagination, we are invited to purposely disperse. To lose ourselves in something much bigger. But not pointlessly. Rather, in dying to our context, we activate it. We become the catalyst that brings flavour, strength, depth, potency and growth. Without yeast, there is no loaf – just dough. Literally, we die to ourselves for growth. We are the ingredient that makes bread for the world.

But this is not a call to dying or dissolving. God wants us alive, not dead. (Actually, the more alive the better!) So the notion of our ministry is not that we are the yeast per se, but rather that we offer a yeast-like-type ministry. It is about being the agent of transformation that is often small, or even unseen. It is about being immersed so deeply in the world and the parish that the depth of growth is often unquantifiable. As Einstein once said, that which truly counts in life can seldom be counted. The work of yeast is one of intensive and extensive growth.

Baking bread, if you have ever done it, is rewarding work and very therapeutic. But it also offers us a rich analogy for what we are about. John Paul Lederach, in his *Moral Imagination*,[9] offers a rich meditation on our calling to be yeast. Consider this: the most common ingredients for making bread are water, flour, salt, sugar and yeast. Of these, yeast is the smallest in quantity, but the only one that makes a substantial change to all the other ingredients. Lederach says you only need a few people to change a lot of things.

So yeast, to be useful, needs to move from its incubation and mixed into the process, out of the seminary and into the parish. Clergy (like the proverbial manure), do the most good when they are spread around. But yeast also needs to grow; it requires the right mix of moisture, warmth and sugar. And it initially needs covering and cultivating before it is ready to do its work. (The analogy for training and formation could hardly be more fruitful here.) Only then should the yeast mix with the greater mass. In bread, it is kneaded into the dough; it requires a bit of muscle. And it also requires someone else to light the fire to make the oven. Bread, in other words, is not just about the yeast, but about a context, one of feeding, desire, need, and the skills of others. So in talking about small fungi that produce change and growth, Jesus is asking us to imagine his kingdom, one in which tiny spores mixed in to the social mass can make a huge difference. One of my predecessors at Cuddesdon, Robert Runcie, had this to say about classic parochial ministry:

Confronted by the wistful, the half-believing and the seeking, we know what it is to minister to those who relate to the faith of Christ in unexpected ways. We do not write off hesitant and inadequate responses to the gospel. Ours is a church of the smoking flax, of the mixture of wheat and tares. Critics may say that we blunt the edge of the gospel and become Laodicean. We reply that we do not despise the hesitant and half-believing, because the deeper we look into human lives the more often we discern the glowing embers of faith.[10]

Similarly, Jesus also invokes his disciples to be the salt of the earth: 'You are the salt of the earth; but if salt has lost its taste, how can its saltiness be restored? It is no longer good for anything, but is thrown out and trampled under foot.'[11]

In interpreting this text, most preachers and many Bible commentaries work with a false assumption: that the salt in this text is the white granular chemical we know as sodium chloride, normally found in a condiment set or kitchen cupboard, where its purpose is to add flavour to foods, or occasionally to act as a purifier or preservative.

Yet the fact that Jesus refers to the salt of the earth ought immediately to alert us to another meaning for the text. The salt (*halas*) mentioned in the text is hardly likely to be table salt, since it is a chemical and culinary improbability that sodium chloride will lose its flavour. Any salt that is extracted from food, water or any other substance remains salty; even if it loses its form, it retains its essence, as many a spoilt meal and frustrated chef can bear witness.

The substance of Jesus' words are, in Greek, *to halas tes ges*, the salt of the earth, with the word for 'earth' here not referring to the world at all, but rather to soil. In other words, the salt that Jesus is referring to here is probably a kind of salt-like material or mineral such as potash or phosphate. These *halas* elements were available in abundance in and around the Dead Sea area of Palestine, and were used for fertilizing the soil and enriching the manure pile, which was then spread on the land.

There are further clues as to why our usual understanding of this text is in some respects flawed. The word 'taste' that features in most English versions of this passage is actually a poor translation of the Greek word *moranthe*, which literally means to become foolish. (The English word 'moron' is derived from the term.) A number of translators render the word as tainted, but 'loses its strength' is probably the best way to translate the word: loss of strength and foolishness would have been synonymous in Jesus' age. Moreover, and ironically, although paved paths also have their uses, Jesus' salt is arguably never useless.[12]

The soil, of course, contains many different elements, all of which are intertwined. Soil, then, is a kind of cipher for the particular cultural contexts (religion, culture, ideology) in which Christians are to be salt. The many soils of the world carry, in various degrees, qualities of empowerment and disempowerment within cultures. Moreover, in a post-modern world, we can now see that culture is being increasingly homogenized through globalization, which has brought with it materialism, individualism, consumerism and hedonism, with the undesirable result of suffocating the life-giving force of the earth.

The empowering mission of the church, like the salt of Jesus' parable, has a consistency of power. However, that power, enculturated into contexts, does not result in uniformity. Rather, it leads to considerable diversity of expression, growth and human flourishing. The salt has always to respect the type of earth in which it is situated, and diverse cultural sensibilities have to be taken into account in the mission of the church. The soil can also be inhospitable: it may be rocky, thorny, and adversely affected by climatic conditions. Under these circumstances, the task of being the salt of the earth is more demanding.

A key to understanding the relationship between church and culture rests on a tension. On the one hand, Christians are to be engaged in the world and influence it, perhaps in ways that are not easily identified as specifically Christian. The power of salt is that it is pervasive, and nourishing. Here, the church accommodates culture; Christ is therefore, in some sense, *for* culture. On the other hand, Christianity also proclaims God's kingdom, a radically other culture that will sweep away the present order. This is the beacon of light set on the hill: it illuminates the present, but points to a new order. This is the Christ who is above or against culture. The church seeks a kingdom that is to come, and it therefore resists the standards of the world.

Accommodation and resistance are, of course, closely related. What they share, in character, is resilience. We might say that accommodation is a soft form of resilience – flexible, pliable, adaptable and so forth – while resistance is a hard form of resilience – concrete, unyielding and defiant. The true character of ecclesial resilience, construed in almost any local church context, will show that most congregations will simultaneously resist and accommodate culture. The church, albeit unconsciously for the most part, understands that it lives between two cultures.

This way of understanding the *halas* (salt) of Jesus' metaphor changes the sense of the text significantly. In fact, it completely undermines the most conventional translations and expositions. The salt is not to be kept apart from society, and neither is it to be used as a purifier or as an additive stabilizer. Ministers are not to be simply preservers of the good society, and neither are they merely agreeable folk adding flavour to either an amoral or immoral society. More powerfully and positively, true religion, as salt, is a life-bringing force giving itself to an otherwise sterile culture.

Thus, the salt of Jesus' metaphor is a mutating but coherent agent that is both distinct yet diffusive in its self-expenditure. As a result of individuals, communities, values, witness and presence, the *halas*, being literally dug into society, the earth or soil, will benefit, and many forms of life can then flourish. Correspondingly, salt that loses its strength (rather than its flavour, the more usual translation) is only suitable for making paths, as the biblical text confirms. Thus, the salt of Jesus' metaphor is not only counter-cultural; it enriches the earth and many more things besides, by being spread around and within it.

So there is an irony here. The task of the salt is not necessarily to maintain its own distinctiveness, but rather to enrich society through diffusiveness. There is also a temporal dimension here: what must begin as distinct to be useful ends up being absorbed and lost. Of course, this reading of the metaphor makes sense of Jesus' own self-understanding, which in turn is reflected in his parables, teachings and other activities. So, if the church or the disciples of Jesus are the salt of the earth, they will begin by being a distinct yet essential component within society, but who will ultimately fulfil their vocation by engaging self-expenditure.

What, then, are the practical implications for training and formation in rural ministry arising from these two organic metaphors? Three brief points can be made by way of conclusion. First, the yeast is suggestive insofar as it reminds churches and ministers that Christianity is about change and conversion, but that such transformation is often natural and organic, rather than traumatically disruptive. Nonetheless, the church is to be a catalyst, not a catacomb. Second, the salt suggests that a patient vocation of nourishing lies at the heart of many rural ministries. To actively engage in the nourishment of the soil is to be committed to a time-consuming and costly process that will *not* yield instant results. Moreover, the 'salting' of the soil is about broad coverage, a deep and extensive parochial exercise rather than something solely concentrated in congregations or in confessional particularity. Third, ministers need to develop a wisdom that can both resist and accommodate culture, but set within a broader understanding of how the church (and its tradition, the gospel, etc.) remains fundamentally resilient. Training in colleges, courses and in post-ordination schemes therefore needs to continually develop forms of theological reflection that help ministers surface the tensions and changes that are part and parcel of rural life. It also needs to equip ordinands to be animators and mobilizers in mission, as well as providing pastoral enablement and consistency. The call for clergy is, in other words, to be agents of change as well as continuity. For both change and continuity are at the heart of the gospel, just as they are the very centre of good, balanced rural mission and ministry.

And finally, to return to Elmdon. This is a community that is seemingly unchanged, and yet now enjoys a plethora of identities. And arguably it has never been broader in its composition: the inhabitants ranging from commuters, to those working more locally, to those who have retired to the village because of its relative proximity to Cambridge. It has also been ministered to as a single community, and now as part of a team, and with ordinands from nearby theological colleges adding to richness now provided by readers, non-stipendiary clergy, associate and retired priests, as well as the laity and other kinds of support.

It is ironic that this new breadth and emergent diversity in Elmdon, seen by 'real villagers' as the apparent fragmentation of its true identity, that now presents the church with a fresh opportunity: to be the gathering place in a community that needs to find new and old purpose in being knit together; to bring locals and strangers together; to foster relations between established families and newcomers; to create a genuine community of worship that expresses the complexity and richness of the parish, in its emerging composition. Kinship is indeed at the core of this. But it is the kind of kinship of the kingdom that Jesus speaks of that is to be fostered; something in the world, but not exactly of it.

Questions

1 Who should take responsibility for cultivating the yeast and the salt in rural ministry, ensuring it flourishes so that the community is cared for and evangelized?

2 Is there room for strategy alongside a patient and organic approach to ministry?

3 What insights and stories might inform the work of theological education (in colleges, courses and continuing ministerial

development) in the response to the vision for organic, exten-sive and patient husbandry in ministry in rural contexts?

Notes

1 Marilyn Strathern, *Kinship at the Core: An Anthropology of Elmdon*, Cambridge: Cambridge University Press, 1981.

2 Jean Robin, *Elmdon: Continuity and Change*, Cambridge: Cambridge University Press, 1980.

3 For further discussion, see David Clark, *Between Pulpit and Pew*, Cambridge: Cambridge University Press, 1982.

4 David Martin, *On Secularization: Towards a Revised General Theory*, Aldershot: Ashgate, 2005.

5 Text from a Cuddesdon student T-shirt.

6 James Hopewell, *Congregation: Stories and Structures*, Philadelphia: Fortress Press, 1987, p. 11.

7 Karl Barth, *Church Dogmatics*, IV, ii, Edinburgh: T & T Clark, 1958, chapter 15, p. 648.

8 Matthew 13.33.

9 John Paul Lederach, *The Moral Imagination*, Oxford: Oxford University Press, 2005.

10 Robert Runcie, 'Comment', *Church Observer*, June 1962.

11 Matthew 5.13.

12 For a fuller discussion of this passage, see V. G. Shillington, 'Salt of the earth?', in *The Expository Times*, Edinburgh: T & T Clark, vol. 112, no. 4, January 2001, pp. 120–2. See also Luke 14.39. Interestingly, *The New Jerusalem Bible* (London: Dartman, Longman & Todd, 1985) is the only modern translation that renders the Greek correctly with 'you are the salt *for* the earth'.

Index